Modern Art

by

Heather Parsons

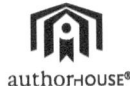

authorHOUSE®

AuthorHouse™
1663 Liberty Drive, Suite 200
Bloomington, IN 47403
www.authorhouse.com
Phone: 1-800-839-8640

First published by AuthorHouse 8/28/2007

ISBN: 978-1-4343-2361-3 (sc)

Printed in the United States of America
Bloomington, Indiana

This book is printed on acid-free paper.

Modern Art

By

Heather Parsons

This book is dedicated to all the darker aspects in life that not only make living that much more interesting, but make the light that trickles in that much more cherished. Also, thank you to the free-thinkers out there, for all the people who dare to be different and are anything but sheep. As for the sheep? "Baa, baa".

This story is also dedicated to all of my friends and family who have cheered me on through each step in this journey. Not to mention an exceptional thanks to all those who gave me a reason to smile.

And mostly, this book is dedicated to my mom for having supported me since the beginning and for having always believed in me. Also, this dedication goes to my dad for being my strength and knowing just how to make all the fine points click into place. And of course, a dedication to my little brother for not being one of the many sheep.

AUTHOR'S DISCLAIMER

The contents in this book are purely fictitious and not based on any persons living or dead—especially dead. The material within is extremely graphic and meant for mature audiences only. Aka, this is not some kiddie Disney bedtime story, folks. Reader discretion is strongly advised.

P.S. Just keep in mind, it's only a book, so if it becomes too intense? PUT THE FUCKING BOOK DOWN.
Thank you.

"All my life I've always wanted to see something terrible happen to someone else, like being brutally killed in a violent car wreck.
I guess I got tired of waiting in rush hour traffic."

-Sam Ellis

"I found the secret to life, I'm okay when everything is not okay."

-Tori Amos

"The art life is… it's just another way of saying the great life."

-David Lynch

1

2:37 AM

It didn't matter that she couldn't see me. Sometimes it's better that way--but only in the beginning. It really didn't matter. The lights were dimmed just so, kinda' like the way the older movie theatres dimmed their lights. She didn't seem to mind—after all we were, just having fun. That's what she said believe me, countless times as a matter of fact. I watched her from that dark spot I had nestled into, and she moved like some swirling ribbon in the wind. She danced perfectly in a dimly lit room—dancing just for me. Only for me.

Like'em like that, I like'em like that. First that tight little fucking shirt came off, and that grin was worn so perfectly on her lips. Full fucking lips. She danced, carrying some secret within her it seemed. Would she share that with me? I have to admit that I shifted in my chair some; I was getting antsy just watching that body of perfection move in front of me.

She giggled. Hesitated.

"Keep going."

She did.   She kept dancing to some idiotic, hypnotic tune that was playing.   A CD I had bought a few years ago because the girls seemed to like it.   Girls have a tendency to like anything shiny, sparkly, or catchy —that CD was all of the above, apparently.   Although, I guess she didn't care about how catchy and sparkly that CD was.   She was a bit fucked up, a bit boozed up, a bit heated up.   She wanted me.   I guess I wanted her to want me.   Next those jeans were un-zipped, slowly.   A hand slid down, so soft and slender… nails tugging at the silvery zipper, making it peel open.

I'd like to see her panties.   See them soaked.   See the wet cunt…and yet, there were no panties.   Another giggle.

"Surprised?"   She asked, her speech rather intact.   I guess a heavy drinker would have the slurring under control by now.   Her jeans fell about her ankles, revealing soft, supple legs.   Once again, I shifted in my seat.   Had she seen me?   Not yet.

"Keep going."

"Naw.   I should head off. I'm so fucked up. I'm gonna' call a cab or something."

"Keep going."

She stopped, those shapely hips of hers halted dead in their tracks now.   She stared in my general direction.   "Do you have a phone?" She stumbled now closer to me.

"Yes."

"C'n I borrow it?"

Okay, so she slurred slightly.   Her breasts swayed as she stumbled forward.   I watched her silently now, mesmerized by the full figure of that woman in front of me.   Her nipples pert, hard.   Her stomach pouting out slightly over full hips cocked to the side, and the slightest of pubes around her fine little tight cunt.

"Yes, as long as you keep going."

"Look, I don't mind fucking around like this, but I really don't *do* things with chicks…it's just not my thing, okay?"

"Maybe a few more drinks?"

Another laugh. This time I was able to pick up on a slight nervousness coming from her.

"Naw, where's your phone?"

I sighed, I wasn't even really wet yet. Then again, I knew that would be the case. I knew it would be. Her full curves stood out in the dim, vermilion glow of my bedroom. I pulled my hand away from my jean-clad pussy and slid it beneath me. Underneath me sat my helper. My cock.

A click.

She froze.

"What was that?"

Though of course that noise sounded an awful lot like a gun clicking. The bitch was smart, even while inebriated. She clearly could handle her drinks well. I have to admit, I'm a bit envious. I lifted my gun up now. It was fully cocked and loaded. Had I been a man, it was my fucking cock, and I would pump her with my seed in an instant. Although, I would hate to put bullet holes in her pretty little flesh.

"First…keep going."

"You're kidding, right?"

I aimed my gun at her head. The click of the chamber echoed louder than the music ever could've been. "Keep going."

And now with the glint of steel aimed at her, her intuition, even if it was a bit fucked up, knew I wasn't kidding. She continued to move, though her rhythm was thrown off. It wasn't as smooth…not as rich. It was forced, and rightly so, it should be. After all, I'd be a bit timid to move if a gun were aimed at me while I danced. Nevertheless, she moved. With my free hand I began to stroke my pussy once more, trying to wake the old girl up. And yet, inevitably, I knew there was no rousing her until I roused another beast.

I was getting quickly tired of this game.

I sighed and stood up.

"Now I can stop? I mean, this really isn't funny, okay? I just need to make a ca...actually wait, never mind. I can just walk, it's cool. I r--please? Please! Oh GOD PLEASE! OH FUCKING CHRIST PLEASE!"

I was berating her. The back of my gun slamming into her face, making blood sling out like when you flick water from your hands after washing them. I hit her. Again. Again. Again. The crack of her teeth against the metal of my gun. My fucking gun. My cock. I hit her over and over. She couldn't stumble back too far since my bedroom wall was behind her. Her blood created delicate splotched patterns on my wall. The wall flowers. She slumped to the floor now.

"Please…please…oh God please…"

I placed the nozzle of my gun, my cock, under her chin. She shut up. Tears of hers intertwined with that blood that now fell freely from her face. I couldn't see the damage inflicted upon her beauty entirely. A swollen eye? A broken nose? It looked like pulp from a mashed grapefruit. Or tomato. She lifted her head up, complying with the cold feel of

steel from my cock beneath her chin.
"Suck me," I whispered now beside her ear.
Sobbing was the response I got.
"Suck me so hard 'til I cum." I hissed now.
I shoved my cock between her lips, forcing
her to take my shaft right in. My free hand
slid about her throat. "Suck me! SUCK ME
OFF!"
And she did. She sucked my cock, her lips
wrapping about that steel and sucking hard.
She had those sobbing hiccups--I think
they're cute if they're not over done. If
they're over done, it can become incredibly
annoying. She continued to suck...now my
pussy was finally getting wet.
"Atta' girl…" I breathed in deeply. My hand
left her throat and moved back to my now
soaked pussy. I began to stroke it firmly
through my jeans, pushing against it hard.
The old girl was awake. I pushed against it
harder as she sucked.
"Suck it…" I hissed out. "Suck it so hard,
you fucking bitch. Suck it."
And she sucked, sobbing all the while. I
stroked, pushed, breathed…cum, cum, cum!
CUM! I arched back slightly, cumming finally.
Finally. I can't remember if I groaned or
not, but I do know this, I squeezed the
trigger. My cock needed to explode on its
own.
Click.
We came together. She screamed, well,
it was a rather muffled one, but a scream
nonetheless. Not like she died or anything.
I wouldn't really load my cock with bullets…
no way. I pulled my gun out of her mouth,
her sobs were hysterical now. I gathered

myself together, my orgasm a small one.
Nothing like what I knew was to come as I
lifted my arm up, gun in hand.
"Please..." she whimpered, but she had
already given up. Did she even know how
turned on I was by her pathetic cries to no
one? Probably not, fucker. "Please…please...
please..."
The crack of a skull is a sound very few get
the pleasure to hear. As the butt of my cock
struck her skull, she passed out cold, that
soft, bruised body slumped on the rug.
I slid my cock back into my jeans then wiped
the small gathering sweat beneath my chin.
A few strands of my hair stuck to my face,
not from my sweat I assumed. Most likely
from her messy, splattering blood. I wrapped
my fingers now about her ankles and dragged
her forward towards my bathroom. I love
the floor plans of my apartment. Everything
was within easy access. She was such dead
weight, especially a girl of her size--not
that she was sickly huge or anything, but she
definitely was of the Marilyn Monroe-esque
build.
I reached my bathroom, my favorite room of
the entire place. Utterly white, sterile,
clean, crystalline. I especially loved the
tub. It was porcelain, modeled after a
tub from the 1930's, as a matter of fact.
Hoisting her up onto my toilet I couldn't
help but think how ecstatic I'd be once I
got an authentic 1930s bath tub complete
with the clawed feet and all. Lovely. The
reproduction worked just fine for the moment—
after all, it served its purpose.
        She was kind of a light-weight compared

to some of the other girls I'd had here
before. Perched on my toilet, her body slid
to the side, leaning severely on the sink
cabinet where I studied her a moment, now in
bright, florescent lighting. Yes, I had done
some severe damage to her pretty face. Blood
streaked over her flesh like red paint on a
white canvas. Her hair was meshed in shades
of blonde, red, and magenta. Her left eye
was beginning to swell up, her lower lip was
split, and it looked like her jaw hung at
some ungodly angle. Blood from the left side
of her head spilled profusely down her face
and shoulders. A work of art.

2

3:34 AM

I watched her for a long time. It's a bad habit of mine. Sometimes I can just sit and stare at them for hours and hours and hours. It's so pretty to me. My favorite part is when they come around. In her case, it would be a little while. She was pretty drunk, and I nailed her hard on the head with my cock. But, her shallow breathing told me she would awaken. I shook myself out of my reverie and stood up from the bath tub's edge. I washed my hands, crusted with her dried blood and of course, myself, then set to cleaning up the floor in my perfectly sterile bathroom, followed by a healthy cleaning of my bedroom.

Getting everything clean didn't take as long as I expected.

I headed to my pride and joy, my tub. I peeled open the shower curtain, exposing an old, extra large, meat hook. It was hanging from my ceiling right above my tub by a metal chain. Thanks E-Bay! It took forever to install it so it could hold up large amounts of weight. I began to run the bath, testing the water to see if it was warm enough. After a few minutes, the temperature was just right.

I turned back to her. She was starting to twitch, as they all usually do. I moved to stand right in front of her, and then slid over her, able to straddle her some on that toilet seat. She uttered a groan and slowly her eyes fluttered open. Bloodshot, glassy, red, lolling--most of their eyes were that way.

She looked at me with the faintest of recognition and when she did, I knew I needed to reward her for that. I leaned in and pressed my lips against hers. She uttered a stifled moan of pain as I begin to kiss her. I guess her jaw was more broken than it looked. I slid my tongue into her mouth, pushing it in so far and deep. She couldn't do much to fight back or even respond back. But that was okay…I was kissing her, not the other way around.

God forbid it.

I then pulled away, my teeth tugging on her lower lip at first playfully until another bad habit of mine kicked in. I tugged now, harshly, biting down as hard as possible and then pulled back, taking a chunk of her flesh with me. I now had her perfect lips—well her bottom lip, anyway. So perfect. She cried out with the little strength she had. I'm sure it was in agony. I was in ecstasy.

My hands then found their way about her throat and slammed her head against the back of the wall, the small of her back crashing against the porcelain support of the toilet. I began to squeeze that precious throat of hers.

Tight.

Tighter.

Tighter…

Her eyes began to bulge out--no, more like bug out. She began to gasp for air as little gurgling sounds came from within. Her hands lifted up to my back, nails pushing into my flesh through my shirt. I didn't mind. Others had put up more of a fight than this. I squeezed harder. She jerked spontaneously beneath me, struggling and striving to get those last few breaths into her screaming lungs. Her hands dropped. I watched her face turn a pretty shade of robin's egg blue. Her lips were almost the color of that one girl who turned into a blueberry from the movie, *Willie Wonka and the Chocolate Factory*.

"Violet, you're turning violet, Violet!"

Yeah, that scene--speaking of which, Gwenyth Paltrow will be on *Access Hollywood* tonight discussing children's books. I needed to tape it.

And just as her bulging eyes suddenly closed, and her body went incredibly limp, I released.

She coughed. I could feel the palpitations of her heart thrashing wildly, like some scared little rabbit. And she slumped back, now no breath came from her lips at all. I leaned in close, pressing, smearing my lips over her own bloodied ones, and forced another kiss. This was a different kiss entirely though. I blew air into her, pumped, and blew in more air.

Blow.

Pump.

Blow.

Pump.

Jerking forward, she coughed and sputtered as she revived from the lack of oxygen. She gasped, coming around now, her body shaking violently from the severe shock it was in, poor thing. More tears fell down her cheeks…or was that blood? I wasn't sure at this point. I was too busy grinding against her, my pussy throbbing for more attention.

She uttered something in such a hoarse voice I couldn't make it out the first time she said it.

"Hm?"

"Ppp...please…I don't…don't wanna…don't wanna die. Oh God please…"

"No, no..." I said now against her, my eyes making sure to keep a strong contact with hers. "*God* isn't choosing to kill you now. He's not. Know why? Because..."

My hand found its way around her throat once more and began to squeeze. A small heaving sound came from within her. She was going to vomit, I knew this kind all too well. I really disliked it when they did that. As I squeezed her, dry heaves were brought up now, all that she had consumed within the past four hours or so. Vomit covered my hands, blood seemed to come up as well… then again, maybe she didn't throw up blood, perhaps it was the blood she was already losing down the side of her face mixing in with her vomit. Whatever it was, I continued to squeeze harder, making her eyes bulge once again. That familiar blue starting to come back. That heart pounded madly, wildly…and I was straining to see that look in those bulging eyes of hers. Come on.

"...because," I continued, vomit or no vomit on my hand. She began to jerk beneath me, somehow her eyes able to meet my own. "*I* am choosing to kill you. I am killing you. *I* am

12

God. I am making the decision that you are to die now…not Him. *I* am. Me." I squeezed even harder, and her shaking stopped now. Her eyes rolled back, showing only glassy whites, her tongue stuck out of her mouth like a dead fish floating to the top of the lake. Her lips looked beyond swollen, her face held that same shade of light blue. She slumped completely beneath me, and was utterly silent, lying, or should I say, sitting in her own blood and puke. Disgusting.

I slid off of her, my pussy now aching, and rubbed my crotch through my tight jeans. I rubbed frantically, furiously…CUM dammit!

RELEASE!

…Sometimes the old girl can dominate me more than I'd care to admit. I looked to the work of art on my toilet. Not finished. Missing something. I leaned over and hoisted her carefully over my slender shoulder. She was heavy, but not the heaviest. I spun about on the heel of my boot and stepped towards my bathtub. I arched up and slung her forward onto the sharp end of that overly large fish hook. It served its purpose well, sinking deep into her back with a sickening, slick, sucking sound. And there she hung like wet laundry to dry. She looked as limp as a rag doll, vomit and blood slowly filling the bathtub. The water was staining a bright red color as she swung slowly above it, feet, hands, and head dangling almost comically—Charlie Chaplin style.

It was then I realized either I hadn't choked her completely, or her nerves took a while to go off, because she began to tremor and jerk on the hook, making heaving sounds

once more. More like gurgles, spittle mixed
with blood dripping down from her lips. Mucus
leaking out her nose, and from where the hook
penetrated into her back, a drizzle of blood
fell down. I loved my '30's bathtub. It
caught everything. I stood back, watching her
wriggle like a worm on a hook until she was
finally still, then stepped forward and gripped
her shoulders. I shoved her down harder on
the hook, and with a sickening "pop" the steel
of the hook came out through and between her
breasts. A bit of the spinal column had gotten stuck on the hook as I pushed it through
her, piercing her like some sort of cannibal's
version of a shish kabob. More twitching, but
it was only slight--nerve endings.

She relieved herself, shit coming out wet
and runny down her cunt and legs, urine following afterwards. Like I said, I loved my
bathtub even more in that moment. I stopped
the running water, and let her hang there to
dry. I was tired. This had taken a lot out of
me. I needed to rest, and in a few hours I'd
come back to check up on her.

3

5:16 AM

I didn't rouse from my bed when I heard that damn CD skip. I was never a fan of music anyway, and CDs didn't add to my opinion either. I hated the way they would scratch or skip from the smallest of things, such as dust. They were a pain, but the girls seemed to like them. Girls like anything shiny, I'd come to find out. But to be honest, I wasn't entirely concentrating on music at the moment.

I hugged my pillow and sobbed. No wait, not sob, I bawled. I cried like when a child gets lost in Disneyland and is separated from its mother, and then is berated by strangers right and left. I cried. I dropped my face into my pillow, choking the sobs into my throat, trying to shut up, and I just couldn't.

I knew this was going to happen. I knew it from the moment I picked her up. It happens every time, and I can't explain why. Sure, I'm a sick fuck. I'm messed up by all assessments, in every way a human being could be. I'm deranged, homicidal, a killer, a monster--and I know it. Kinda brings you back to the question, does an insane person know that they're actually insane? I'd like to say yes, but wouldn't that be incorrect since insanity is defined as the absence of all logical thinking? And I'd like to think of myself as pretty damn logical.

For instance: You're cold, put on a sweater. The light is too bright, turn it off. You're sick, go to a doctor. Except, I doubt there are any doctors that can fix the kind of condition I've got.

Actually, let me think back…did I always bring a date home to slaughter, literally? Yes actually, I guess I did, now that I think of it. Don't ask me to justify it. I'm sure that'll come in time. For now, let me fucking cry. Let me cry because yes, I know there's something drastically wrong with me. Drastically wrong with playing "God"…drastically wrong with choking the life out of a girl, slitting her up from the cunt to her mouth, watching her intestines and ovaries spill out like a waterfall of organs. I love it. I love it so much, oh Christ I love it.

I rolled over, tears brimming in my eyes. I had a guest waiting for me in the shower, and a CD that was skipping like mad. Finally I sat up, my mascara, I was sure, down to my cheeks Tammy Faye Baker style and my hair probably a tangled mess, but, first thing's first. I stood up and headed to my stereo. I clicked the button, stopping that incessant, horrid sound and then glanced towards the bathroom. I heard complete and utter silence, listening to see if I might hear anything else. Now if I did, *that* would have been scary, like something right out of a Stephen King movie.

I decided to leave my guest in the bathroom for now. I needed to check on one other. I stepped out of my room. The rest of my apartment was just as clean and as sterile as my bathroom. No carpet, only tile—easier to clean and to keep clean. All my furniture of course is designed and created by none other than me. My place, my humble abode was my work creation, my life, my ultimate masterpiece. The girls I brought here? Eventually, all of them became the works of art to help forge this magnificent conception. My apartment was not only my home, but it was my continual magnum opus—living tissue becoming immortalized through my perfectly crafted touch. My décor mainly consisted of steel to reflect the beauty that is me and my work, as well as marble, and of course, the personification as well as crafted integration of my girls.

I walked silently through the kitchen and towards the guest room. It had been nearly twelve days since I had been in there last. I think. Honestly, I had a lot on my mind, you know? What with going to work, socializing, cleaning, paying bills… it gets one kinda' busy at the moment.

Silently, I stepped into the guest room, it was dark--just the way I liked my lighting. The guest bed was neatly made, the floors vacuumed, the window was washed--everything perfect…except for the smell. And oh God, what a stench. It was reeking from the closet just where I left her. I covered my nose with the back of my hand, lightly smelling the apple hand soap I used to wash my hands with earlier. I stepped lightly to the closet door and opened it slowly.

Art.

She sat there, a glazed expression on her

face, though it took no doctor to tell that she was dead--long dead. Her skin had turned from a healthy rosy peach color to a now pallid grey. Her flesh was wrinkling up, rigor mortis had left her clearly, she lay as limp as a rag doll on the floor. Bodily juices had leaked from her like when you leave an ice cream sandwich out in the sun too long. That grey flesh was peeling in some areas on her face. The handcuffs she wore about her slender wrists appeared to have left bruises--the coloring of her skin in that area was a strange banana yellow and plum purple color.

Like I said, art.

Her eyes remained halfway open, the whites only showing. Some sort of green fluid, perhaps a mixture of the eye gunk and mucus, seemed to be leaking down her hallowed cheeks. She looked utterly thin, utterly malnourished. That tends to happen when you don't eat for such a long time. Cause of death: Starvation.

Wait a second...down on her forearms looked to be grooves dug furiously out of the skin, bits of her skin were ripped up. I knelt down, still covering my nose from the smell. I glanced at her hands...beneath her dull, darkened nails were bits of flesh. I blinked a few times-- had she clawed her own flesh off? Why? I stepped back some, and then it clicked. I noticed in her mouth were a few bits of grey flesh hanging like limp hooks from her lips. She was...eating herself? Well, I guess if you were desperate enough...

I surveyed the rest of her, her tits seemed to sag down, deflated. Her stomach paunch seemed to cave in, pearl colored stretch marks were riddled all about her decayed form. A clear fluid leaked from her vagina, the pubic hair was dampened and pushed against her peeling flesh. I had to take another step back now, the stench was bad. And yet…after seeing her this way? Jesus fucking Christ, I was wet. So fucking wet. I've sent some of the girls into the closet before, making them starve-- hearing their moans of pure hunger at two or three in the morning and got off. But, none had gotten me so turned on like this girl... how desperate could she have been?

How much could she have relied on me to feed her? Keep her alive? How much she needed something…what were her last thoughts? What was she thinking as she felt her stomach and intestines turn in on themselves, consume herself from within with her stomach acid? Did she even feel the pain she gave herself by trying to eat her own flesh? Did she? Did she?

I was on the guest bed now, my hand down my jeans, beneath my panties, furiously rubbing my clit. So wet… so wet like the juices that leaked from her dead carcass. With a groan of pure satisfaction, I came. I came so hard my teeth chattered. I love mid-morning orgasms- -they seem to be so much more stimulated than night ones, or mid-afternoon ones. I pulled my sopping, wet hand from my pants, my juices dripped down my fingers, shakily climbed to my feet and staggered over to her dead body. The smell was still bad, but it was as if I was in a trance and couldn't care less. I knelt down, her juices soaking through the knees of my jeans and I could feel her wetness on me as I leaned forward. I slipped my fingers into

19

her mouth now, and she complied with me so simply. Like some doll. I let her taste me--she could eat as much as she wanted now.

I grew wet once more, having my fingers within her mouth, her tongue felt like sandpaper, everything was so cold, like ice. It was a bit wet, most likely from the bile that had backed up in her throat. I shoved two fingers in her mouth while I (and believe me, I couldn't help it) shoved three fingers of my own, back into me. She was the best fuck I had ever endured.

Once my second orgasm had me spiraling into a land of sheer ecstasy, I stood up and cleared my throat.

"Thanks darlin'."

She didn't look up at me when I spoke. In fact, she didn't look at anything.

"Now, that's rude." I said with a disappointed tone. I leaned back down and I placed the tips of my fingers on her actual eye ball and made them roll back to look somewhat at me. I used to always wonder if pupils remained dilated or not when someone died. They are beyond dilated. I got my question answered. One eye seemed a bit cocked to the side, such pretty brown eyes, even if she wasn't really focused on me.

"That'll do, darlin'." I stood up now, hands on my slender hips. I glanced about the guest room. "Well, shall we grab some breakfast?"

Silence.

"Fine, if you want me to make up your mind for you, I will. Breakfast time it is." I pulled a small silvery key from my pocket and unlocked the cuffs that had been chained to the wall, her hands, and her feet. She was allowed zero mobility with the tight way I had her locked up. Carefully I slid my hands about her slender, icy cold waist. I could feel the slosh of her internal organs, all of her muscles had relaxed completely. I lifted her up and hoisted her over my shoulder just as I had done with the girl last night.

Wet plops of bodily juices sloshed to the floor. Tsk-tsk, another mess I'd have to clean up. She laid like a sack of potatoes over my shoulder, lumpy, unmoving, slightly stiff—malleable in all the right ways. I walked out of the guest room, droppings of wet whatever falling as I left. I headed for my utterly clean kitchen. I had finished paying bills last night, so luckily my kitchen table was completely cleaned off. It's always nice to show off a silvery-metallic table imported from Sweden. I dropped her body atop the flat, smooth surface, making that sick, wet, dull thud as it hit the shiny chrome. Chrome that allowed me to see the reflection of myself as I worked my magic over that rotted, beautiful corpse.

I wiped my hands off on the back of my jeans. I would have some laundry to do later anyway. Thank god I had taken work off today. I loved my days off. I usually spent them like this, cleaning up after the party. I glanced over the naked, grey form on my table. Her dark brown locks of hair looked rather washed out, dull. I wouldn't be keeping those. I headed into my kitchen drawer and pulled out a pair of stainless steel scissors meant for cutting through meat. I suppose I was using them the way they had been intended to be used, right?

I walked back over to the girl's corpse and began to cut her hair off. Lock after lock fell silently to my kitchen floor and looked as if it were some sort of bizarre snow storm. Soon I had cut all I could. For as much as I hated music, I didn't mind hearing the sound of my own voice.

"Okay darlin', the haircut looks smashing."

Does it really? I envisioned her answering back. Though I knew her lips didn't move once.

I was hoping you could rip out some of these pesky intestines, actually. She answered back--in my mind, of course. Like I said, I, at least, understood logic.

"They're bothering you, huh? Guess maybe that's what you get for devouring so much of your own skin."

I know, I was naughty.

"Yes, yes you were."

Please take them out. Please?

"Well…only because you asked nicely. But, just this once, okay?"

It's a deal, Sam.

"Hey!" I suddenly shouted violently. (I had a tendency of losing my temper at times.) "Don't *ever* call me that! EVER!"

Okay…

She was silent now. It was one thing to talk to my girls, but it was another thing entirely when they addressed me by name. I hated that. It made things so… personal. And really, I guess, in a sense, it wasn't. It wasn't personal. It was…art. They were my canvases and I was the artist--no names ever needed to be used. Sure, they would give me their name and that was fine, and most of the time they would be so drunk and horny, they wouldn't give two flying fucks about my name. I liked it that way.

I'm sorry.

"Forget it."

What about my intestines?

I sighed and then headed over to my wooden block filled with cleavers. I pulled one out and stepped over to the girl lying so still on my table. It was like some utterly fucked up version of *Snow White*--minus the glass coffin. I licked my lips and looked her over, deciding where to make such an incision. I stopped, I couldn't think clearly until I had a drink. I walked over to my fridge and pulled out a Snapple--I loved the apple flavored ones. Come to think of it, apple was my favorite of everything. Apple flavor, apple scent, apple red anything apple. I popped the lid open and took a long swig. I wiped my lips with the back of my hand and resumed to work.

I stepped around the table and looked her over. "You lost quite a bit of weight."

I haven't been eating much lately, I guess.

"I'm not a fan of anorexics, you know."

Really? Thin's not in?

"Well, only to a certain point. I don't want some fucking fat cow, mind you. But, a little waif does absolutely nothing for me either," I answered pointedly, placing the tip of the knife on her upper abdomen, a few inches above the naval, then pressing the knife in. With a squishing sound, it sliced deeply within. Thank god the blood was coagulated by now, for that would've been a real mess had it not been clumped together. Believe me, I've had *that* happen to me before. *That*, once being the time I had a girl atop this table, just like now, and I had cut into her a little too quickly. Her blood practically spurted up at me fire hose style—staining my walls and my counter tops. Nice. Or, let's not forget the, "Hey-I'm-Still-Hanging-On-To-Life" chick. I was sure this girl had been suffocated completely before I started to cut into her, so I began to work. She woke up on my table, with a scream to make my ears bleed, her blood sloshing everywhere. I had already made a few cuts into her when she sat up, her intestines did as gravity told them to do. They fell right out. I guess survival instinct kicked in, or the girl was still pretty fucked up, or maybe she had a strong stomach, (no pun intended) but she did her best to scoop them back up. The grey, long, lumpy tubes that had tumbled from her slipped out of her fingers, coating them in her own blood. She then promptly fainted back on my table, and died. Well, actually, I think she died before she fainted--that was a lot of blood to lose at once. Anyway, I've learned since then--make sure they are completely dead before cutting.

I slid that knife down, the dead skin making it so easy to slice her open like I was gutting some fish. The stench rose up practically making the white paint from my kitchen walls peel off. As many times as I had done this, you'd think I would have been used to that smell--wrong. I never, ever did like it. I slit her open, bringing that sharpened knife blade all the way down, past her naval, further down, cutting in such a straight, perfect

line. Down, down, down, further down past the
mesh of dark brown, damp pubic hair, all the
way to her natural slit, her cunt. I sliced
her all the way open, the stench rolling out
in thick clouds of sheer disgust. If smell
could have a color, this one would be putrid
green.

I stepped back and took another swig from
my Snapple apple juice. I remembered once
from my high school anatomy class there was a
special kind of cut called anterior oblique--
more commonly known as the "Y-incision". And
kids in high school said that you'd never ap-
ply the things you learned in the classroom to
real life. Haha, fuckers. I preformed this
cut, with an amazing accuracy, if I do say so
myself.

"There darlin', your intestines are ready
for the taking."

Oh thank you, Sam.

"HEY!" I suddenly screamed out, "What the
FUCK did I say about calling me that?!" In my
rage I didn't notice that I had accidentally
spilled over my Snapple bottle. It clanged
to the tiled floor and amazingly enough, didn't
break. It simply spilled apple juice everywhere. "Now look at what you made me do.
Fucking cunt."

It was a mistake!

"Yeah, I'll bet it was you mother fucking
bitch!" Remember that temper I mentioned? I
brought my knife down
right into her stupid chest, cracking through
her sternum, most likely puncturing a lung.

Please!

"Now you beg?! Now you BEG?! What did I
say?!" That knife struck right back down,

this time bringing dark red blood up, splattering it across my shirt. I didn't care. How many times can you accidentally slip and call me by first name? I then reached into that perfect incision I had made and grabbed hold of something cold—more or less room temperature, thick, almost greasy feeling. I yanked it out with my bare fingers. I liked to use gloves when I wasn't really in the mood, but this disobeying bitch put me in the Goddamned mood alright.

I ripped out as hard as I could, pulling out what looked like a seven inch thick piece of bloated, grey yarn. It was doused in blood and some clear substance I assumed was something akin to plasma. I tugged, and it pulled out like a piece of spaghetti, slopping blood all over the floor. The body jerked some with my harsh, violent movements. I then dropped it on my table with a splat.

"How's that feel? Huh? Better, bitch?"

No. I'm so sorry.

"Yeah, you'd better be." I went to wipe my chin from the sweat that had gathered there but stopped myself in the process. I would have almost smeared her blood all over my face. I mean, like I said, I've got a temper, but I'm no savage. I don't wear blood as some tribal ritual or something. Logic, remember?

Well, at least my intestine is out now…

"You calling me whipped?" I cracked a grin towards her dead face. She stared at nothing in particular. "C'mon, that was kinda' funny, right?"

Are you going to freeze it?

"I don't think so. I kinda' ripped the wall lining of your small intestine when I yanked it out."

But you're so good with your hands.

"Flattery, darlin', gets you everywhere." I licked the side of my lip and then instantly wished I hadn't. I tasted a bit of blood on it, and believe me, it wasn't my blood at all. "Damn."

Why don't you like it?

"Blood? Because I'm not some fucking cannibal. Dahmer was all right until I found out he actually started eating some of his boys. That's just…crossing the line, you know? Besides, blood is unsanitary. You ever hear about those groups of people who think they're vampires?"

The cult groups? The ones they show on shows like Ricki Lake?

"Yep. I hope those fuckers all catch AIDS and die. That's so sick, sucking blood, shooting up with blood--whatever. So..."

Unsanitary?

"Exactly. However, once the body has been completely cleaned out, the skin burns nicely. I try and make use of what I've got. I have no real need for intestines, but…"

But?

"Your eyes would make a great addition to the remodeling of my bathroom."

I set to work now. I used a double pronged fork to scoop in around the eye ball and peeled it out. I have ruined many an eye with this method, but this method is also the most accurate. This time I completely lucked out, I got both of her eyes with no problem. I started on the second eye, the first one came out perfectly with a little "pop" sound. The second eye gave a bit more trouble.

As I stuck the fork in, dark, lumpy, red blood gushed forth like some bubbling, chunky brook. I tilted her head, the blood spilling onto the table. I then stuck the fork in further and began to pry up, a sucking sound was heard. The eyes remained white, glossy, and unfocused.

Suppose this is a bad time to mention that I wear contacts, huh?

"No, this is a bad time to get a sense of humor. Shut up and lemme concentrate." I bit down on my lower lip (a habit I obtained sometime around the third grade. Watching Molly Ringwald do it in *The Breakfast Club* drove me wild. I would kill for her lips--literally) and pried further up. More of a sucking sound then finally a pop as the eye came out. Sort of. It was still attached to a long, stringy looking piece of dark red skin. More cold blood washed over my hands as I worked. I grabbed my scissors (thanks mom) and cut it off. Now I had a perfect pair of eyes I would later clean. Now all that was left was the brain. I began to mark around the scalp with my knife, deciding the best place to slice into my girl.

How old are you?

"Why?"

Just making small talk, I guess.

"Twenty-eight. You?"

I was twenty-three.

"Good usage of past tense verbs there. I woulda' been a little worried had you still thought of yourself in the present tense."

I'm dead, not a dumbass.

"Hey, you're making accusations, not me."

Do you have a favorite color?

"Funny that you ask. I enjoy all colors actually. I'm an interior design consultant."

Pretty successful from the looks of it... your place is gorgeous! Very interesting taste with your décor, but still absolutely stunning.

"Yeah, well, I make due. All my décor is designed, created, and put together by me. Makes it that much more special. It helps to be rather handy with tools and have a pretty keen eye for interior decoration and of course, art."

And be pretty fucking hot for another.

"How do you think I land so many girls?"

You're a lesbian?

"Being sassy, huh? I never actually classified myself as such, though society would. I hate labels. I mean, if I were to start labeling every damn little thing, my life would look more organized than an accountant's filing cabinet. I like my freedoms."

Free spirit philosophy?

"Perhaps. I don't know. I just kinda take each day as it comes." I placed my knife carefully above her skull and began to cut. The knife began to slice through the first layer of skin. As the grey flesh peeled back I could see the small, yellowish tinged bumpy fat, and then thin layer of dark red muscle beneath it. Most people would think everything inside the human body was bright red, with blue veins and the like. Not true. I would know from experience. Most things do have a red tinge, but most things are grey...kinda like life I guess. That's my philosophical thought for the day, by the way.

Did you ever get sick while you were doing

this?

"What? The cutting? Naw, I was always kinda into this sorta thing. When I was a kid I used to own this little white kitten. I never named him, my mother bought him for me to keep me company. I guess she felt bad I was an only child or something. Anyway, one day, I was about fourteen or fifteen...somewhere around there, and I took my kitten into my bedroom. My mother was at one of her Mary Kay parties, so I had the house to myself..."

What about your dad?

"Dunno. I never knew him. From what my mother tells me he was 'the asshole her butt seemed to be missing at the time. And soon enough like a piece of shit would, he left as soon as he came.' I guess he was a one time fuck, and badda bing, I was born. I don't really care to know him and if I ever do meet him? We'll sit down for coffee and a biscotti or something. I hold no grudges."

I'd be ticked at my dad if he did that to me.

"Naw, I'm real close with--excuse me, not "real", that's horrid grammar. I'm *really* close with my mother. I'm sure I didn't miss much in my childhood. Anyway, I took my kitten into my room and just...choked it. I watched it die right in my bare hands. Now of course I knew this wasn't normal, I mean, what teen is choking their kitten, you know? But I did. Why? Not because "mommy" molested me when I was young. I actually had a very normal childhood minus a father. I had a normal education, made tons of friends, fucked a few boys, which I realized made me want to vomit each and every time...I mean, I was basically normal.

So why? I can't justify and I can't explain. I did it because I could. Because that little thing depended on me to live...I guess that's when I realized I held the power to take its life. Not "God" that every religion speaks of. Not Him. Me. So I did."

Makes sense.

"That's what I'm saying. Why does anybody do anything? Because they can. Why be kind? Why be smart? Why protect? Why harm? Why love? Why hate? It's all human nature in a sense."

I guess I never thought of it that way.

"I wouldn't advise you to start. You'll end up like me--or, not. You'll simply just end up becoming the end." I laughed there in my kitchen with her, my girl. That was pretty damn funny. I began to peel her scalp back some, exposing a spider web-like muscle tissue over the skull. I licked my lips, damn why did I knock that Snapple over?

Just what are you, exactly?

"I told you, I hate labels. I am me, and that's all there is to it. Call me what you will, but I go by no specific name or genre."

Fine, Sam.

I looked at her for a moment, my gaze was icy cold, I could feel it. "What the *fuck* did I say about that?!" I hissed out through my teeth.

Not to call you by your first name, Sam.

"Shut. The. Fuck. UP!" I raised my knife. "How fucking simple is it!"

Oh c'mon, Sam! *We both know why you hate names! Because you don't want to be one of us,* Sam! *But face it, you are!* "Human nature" *my ass--you* hate *what you are so you let it out on us! I did jack shit to you! I thought you were fucking hot, I wanted to fuck you, maybe later that day buy you lunch, get your number or give you mine and you blew it, Sam!*

"SHUT UP!" I screamed now. I lifted the knife up

(chop!)

and like the Queen of Hearts from *Alice in Wonderland*, it was OFF WITH HER HEAD! I sliced that cunt's head right the fuck off! No fucking bitch talks to me that way, dead or alive!

"You don't know shit! You don't know your fucking ass from you head! Don't even *try* and pretend to analyze me! Besides look at where your prissy little fucking analyzing got you, huh? DEAD! It got you killed! That's where, you little bloody cunt whore! Now what, huh? Come ON! Speak!"

Silence.

Well, actually, I take that back--the only sound that was heard was the dull, smacking "thud" her head made as fell to the floor. More blood splattered. I glanced at her head-less form on my table. The cut had been semi clean--a bit of sheer white bone--her spine actually was sticking out of her neck. Veins or blood vessels drooped down, wrinkled skin now puckered up slightly against the gaping wound I had created, but no new blood flow. Good. Less to clean, and besides I was get-ting sick of her company anyway.

I quickly placed her eyes into a jar I kept by the sink. It was nearly lunch time and I had a lot of cleaning up to do before I could get to my real project of the afternoon--re-modeling my bathroom, the heart and soul of my apartment. After her head had been disembodied, I quickly chopped the rest of her up, arm after arm. Leg after leg, until she was nothing left but a headless torso.

I collected her dismembered pieces and brought them into my bathroom. I then popped in a movie, one of Gwenyth's (as in the one and only Gwenyth Paltrow) to listen to as I worked. For as worked up as that whore had made me, Gwenyth always seemed to calm me down. I stripped the flesh off of those bones and then cleared out whatever left over contents were in my bath tub, giving the bitch I had strung up the hook a gentle push for fun. Swing bitch, swing. I then filled the bath tub up with hot water and some bleach. The bones were then thrown into it to soak.

Finally, I grabbed those garbage bags now filled with soggy rotted flesh, fat, muscle bits, veins, and all those delicious insides of the human body and placed them aside to take out to the trash compactor later to be burned. Once she was all taken care of, I went through and completely cleaned, mopped and sterilized my kitchen.

I mean how sexy is it to have your kitchen smelling like a corpse when you invite someone over? I placed all of my "tools" such as my knife, fork, and scissors into a small bucket of bleach and left them to soak. I took the bags out of my apartment and, with a quick look around to make sure that the coast was clear, I lugged them downstairs. I loved these little cottage units. Each person had an individual place, not those internal apartments where you lived on a certain floor, having to walk-through, some dirty hallway that smelled like

B.O., just to get home to relax. My complex was more or less like a townhouse. Having a place like this made it easier to bring a girl in off the street faster as well.

I especially enjoyed the leaf burnings and trash burnings we were allowed to do. There was a compost heap outside of our complex complete with a compactor. It was downwind, thank God, and that was where most of my trash went. Like now. I chucked the heavy, black garbage bags into the heap, then headed back up to my place. There would be a burning later this evening. Things always seemed to work out for me.

The second I got back into my place, I finished cleaning everything up. I cleaned until my hands ached and my knuckles bled. I didn't stop until everything was as sterilized as possible and the place was utterly spotless. I, myself, wasn't exactly clean. I still had one more girl to deal with. Though that last bitch put me in a rather foul mood.

I was heading back into my bedroom for her when unexpectedly I heard a loud knock at my door. I froze, and I'm sure my own pupils dilated. I wasn't expecting *anyone*. Who the fuck would be here? I headed to my front door and peered out its small peephole.

Holy Jesus, Mary, and Joseph—heh a little phrase I picked up from the natives around this city.

I swear to God my complexion went whiter than the tiles in my bathroom. The fucking PO-LICE were at my door.

Be calm, be calm, be calm...

I tucked a few short locks of black hair behind my ears. Had I cleaned all the blood off of me? Yes, at least off of my skin. But my shirt? I glanced down

FUCK!

Christ no, I didn't! I look like I could be the spokes model for Bloody Mary! I could even dub as Stephen King's *Carrie* on her prom night! I am FUCKED! Royally fucked! My heart leapt against my chest and I swear I could taste a certain anxious bile creeping up my throat.

KNOCK.

KNOCK.

KNOCK.

"Uh! Just a second!" I responded so hoarsely, my voice almost didn't even sound like mine. Normally I was so confident, charismatic, self-assured. Well, not now, fucking damnit. Not now. I looked around and spotted the white afghan on my couch. I snatched it up and wrapped it about myself like a towel. I then kicked off my jeans and cast them to the side. There. Now...I hope, I hope, I... opened the door.

"Hello officer." I said calmly, pulling a smile across my face.

The cop stood there, his eyes sliding up and down my body at least once. I was used to it, men looked me over all the time like a piece of meat. I didn't mind it. Not from them, anyway.

"Good morning, ma'am," he said with a repressed respectful tone.

"What can I do for you? Oh, I'm sorry you *just* caught me out of the shower. So just excuse my current wardrobe."

"Not a problem ma'am. Not like you were expecting us."

That was the understatement of the century.

"Well, how can I help you?"

"To be honest ma'am, we received a phone call about uh…some loud screaming coming here from this address. So I thought I'd stop by and check it out. Is everything okay?" he asked, taking a quick glance around the apartment.

I blinked. What FUCKER called the cops on me? I'll kill them. I'll slice their lips right the fuck off their Goddamn face. I'll...

"Yes sir, officer. Everything's fine. OH, you know, I did find my cat had peed on my lovely Persian rug about ten minutes ago. I kind of have a temper."

This brought a smile to his chapped lips. "A cat, huh? That's why your place smells like morgue--all the disinfectant."

I smirked, "Yeah, I'd rather smell that than cat piss, sorry--pee."

He laughed now. "I hear you there. My daughter just bought a puppy. She's learning to house train the damn thing. Shits everywhere like some leaky hose. The whole place smells of a dog kennel now."

"That's what I'm trying to prevent."

"Makes sense."

"Was that all? I mean, that was what the visit over here was for?"

"Yeah, but...well, I can see everything's okay. Just try and be a little less loud, okay?" He sent me a wink. "And good luck with that cat."

"No problem officer. And trust me, I'll need all the luck I can get."

"Alright then, ma'am. Sorry for being a disturbance to ya, gotta uphold the law and all," he smirked. Was the fucker flirting with me? I held back a shiver.

"Oh yes, I'd hate to think of the kinda mayhem we'd have if not for the men in uniform around. There are a lot of sickos out there."

"Sure are. You have a good day, ma'am."

"I intend to."

With that he spun around and headed back down the stairs. I watched him leave and the second he got back into his car I sucked in a sigh of relief. I closed my door. Whoever the fuck called the cops on me…oh, I would make them get their own. But not now. Now I had a bathroom to remodel.

4

1:43 PM

The next day, after my little "incident" with the officer I had cleaned those eyes I saved, scraped the veins and whatever else skin and fat and muscle clung to them, until they were perfectly round eyeballs. I only needed two more pairs and I'd be complete with my bathroom. You see, I had mentioned my prized 1930's bathtub--it's my love, but I said nothing of my shower. My shower was in a small corner behind my tub. I didn't want to mess with the tub at the moment. My girl was still hanging on her hook, nearly done drying.

My shower had been a three year project. I had specifically paid and requested for cleanly cut plexi glass cubes to place in the walls of my shower. Clear walls, but only so far. Yet, with each and every plexi glass cube I had, I drilled in a total of two holes. Sure, I know how to use power tools, and I know how to do house work. I'm practically the next Martha Fucking Stewart when it comes to house shit. Why else would I be so successful as an

interior design consultant? I know my shit.
I would only have two more cubes to place in
my shower to complete it, after I finished
this one. After I had drilled the two holes
into the plexi glass cube, I gingerly and
delicately dropped one eye ball in each hole.
I then filled the holes up with formaldehyde,
then I sealed it shut tight.

By the way, obtaining formaldehyde is
not as easy as one might think. They don't
exactly sell that at the local drug store.
However, being as charismatic and as charming
as I am? I was able to hit on a mortician
a few months or so ago. I kept her alive
long enough, holding back on my desires, just
so she could sneak some out of her work for
me. I made up some utterly idiotic lie about
wanting to collect insects or something.
She, being a chick who deals with dead people
(lucky whore) didn't think much of it. Once
she got me a few jars, I ridded myself of
her.

I didn't kill her, she hadn't really
fit the look I wanted to keep for my
apartment's décor. She was too thin, rather
intellectual, and way more into me sexually
than I ever was into her. She grossed me
out—but hey, you gotta do what you gotta do
in order to get the things you need, aka, my
lovely, precious formaldehyde.

I placed the cube down on its given
spot, leaving only two more places for the
last two cubes. I had created, within the
course of three years, my own designed wall
for a shower. Of course, I kept this all
hush-hush, mind you. Play the game well and
fly right. All of that bullshit.

Each and every cube held eye balls in it
(real eyes, not fake glass pieces of crap).
It was some neo-modern design. I liked the
idea of always being watched, it suits me.
The entire walls of my shower were filled with
clear plexi glass cubes with two human eyes
in each one. And to finish off my project I
only needed two more pairs.
I liked the idea of that, a shower that
would always watch your back—as you washed
your back! Ha! That was good. Creative,
inventive, artistic. I grinned and then
stepped out of my shower--now I was truly a
mess.
I had slipped back into that blood donned
shirt and my jeans. It didn't matter. I
only had one other girl to see anyway and she
was just "hanging" around with nowhere to go
and no way to get there.
Yeah, I know, bad pun.
I headed to my favorite 1930's tub and pulled
the curtains open. There she was, hanging
like Christmas mistletoe. She was still just
in her panties, that hook shoved so violently
through her chest. Bits of flesh had caught
on the end, her head lolled to the side, her
tongue now as dry as a bone as it stuck out
of her pale blue lips. I sighed, this was a
sight I didn't ever want to get rid of...yet,
I was smarter than that. Human bodies can
leave some pretty odious stenches.
Still, I could get my Polaroid. I stepped
out for a second, and just as quickly
returned with my camera. I raised the camera
to my eye and muttered, "Smile for the
camera, darlin'."
Make sure you get my best side.

41

"So vain." I murmured back, once again breaking that silence with my voice and thoughts. I snapped picture after picture. The corpse hung there beautifully above that tub. How I loved it. Finally, after about six or seven pictures I decided to take her down. I had to hurry now. I had only about two hours until trash burning.

I still needed to shower, get ready, and head to the bars. I loved Saturdays, the bars were always packed. After I took her down, it was the same thing—I extracted the eyes, then beheaded the body.

You heading out tonight?

"You betcha'."

It's Saturday.

"No kidding! Really?!"

Sarcasto-bitch.

"Ha, well I need to head out; I have to finish my shower."

No work today then?

"Nope. I took Friday and Saturday off. Kinda rocks when you have the sort of clout I do in order to do that. Besides, I have given my work my precious talent, the least they could do is let me take off Friday and Saturday."

Hmm, good point. It's gonna be wild at the bars, you know.

"Oh I intend for it to be." I was now busy stuffing her dismembered head into an air tight plastic bag. Coagulated blood dropped silently to the floor as I shoved her head now inside the freezer. It joined the heads of three previous girls.

As for the rest of the body? I quickly cut up what I could—repeating my same methodically long, but rather imperative process of scraping the flesh, dismembering the body, and then stuffed the removed innards, flesh, and such into two large plastic bags. Off for the garbage pit I went. I had about thirty minutes until burning time. Once the bagged body was placed securely among the rest of the trash, I headed back to my apartment. Ready to do some burning, the trash man inconveniently, yet strangely reassuringly stopped to put his gloves on

"How's it goin', m'am?"

I smiled my most gregarious smile. And why wouldn't I? So far, things were going superbly! I was just in a bit of a rush, that's all. "Pretty well, and yourself?"

"Not bad, not bad. Got m'self some new gloves. The last ones melted to m'hands a bit."

"Ooh, ouch."

"Eh, it wasn't really all too bad."

"Well, I appreciate all your hard work. Keep it up." I flashed him another grin and headed back to my apartment. Fuck you, you damn bitch for thinking I was no better than anyone else. Obviously I could blend right in and no one will know, and instantly that sets me apart from *everyone* else. I'm glad I didn't keep your head…and I'm even more glad you burned first. Now, I'm off to go clubbing…

5

10:57 PM

The bar had already been busy for hours. It always was on Saturdays. I saw the line, a mile long before I even entered, sighed and took my place among all the other idiots of the city. I fished about in my low cut jeans for my wallet, and once it was secured I withdrew my ID. To my amazement, the line seemed to be moving pretty quickly--this was always a good thing.

I noticed the multitudes of eyes that were locked on my body--why not? I worked out, maintained a good shape, stayed fit, I deserved a little attention for my body after all, right? Soon, it was my turn to offer my ID. The picture on it was well-placed, not ragged, or ratty like some people's were if they didn't keep their cards in good condition. That was a pet peeve of mine, not keeping my things clean and orderly--it drove me nuts. So sue me, I'm a bit obsessive compul--

Then I saw it.

The entire club was filled with...filled with... what was she doing here? This was impossible...

wasn't it? I stared, my eyes groped around the darkness of the entrance to the bar, sweeping over the many cloned faces of...*Her!*

She was a girl of mine. In fact, not just any girl, but the one I grew extremely pissed at earlier yesterday--the one who knew my name...the one who ate herself.

"Miss?" A voice cut through my sudden shock.

"Huh?"

"You're holding up the line, head in or head out." The bouncer said gruffly. "Pay the thirteen bucks or not."

"Yeah, yeah, yeah...I should be on the guest list anyway." The bouncer looked my ID over again, then checked his list, his deep voice had been a slap in the face. He handed back my card and nodded me good to go.

I slunk in slowly, and glanced around reluctantly, Everyone looked different. I didn't see that dead girl's face everywhere anymore. *That* was strange.

Heh, maybe I was going insane.

I made the best of my night, pushing that small hallucination far back into my mind as I danced, bought drinks at the bar, and flirted with numerous women. I was looking for the one that would catch my eye, and so far, I hadn't seen her. Not yet...

6

4:13 AM

Staggering out of the bar, I was really pissed off. I didn't find anyone I wanted, not a single one of those fucking mother fuckers. I leaned on the wall to catch my balance. So I was a bit boozed up, okay? Not a crime, not a crime at all.

I needed some water badly, I had a headache that would not give up. I think I had a bit too much to drink. I reached the nearest out-door café, and surprisingly it was open--ah, the city night life. It was all a blur from here...

I ordered water, this much was true.

Did I flirt with the young woman behind me? Perhaps, but in all honesty, I was too fucked up to remember.

The next thing I knew through my whirling drunkenness, I was back in my apartment, lying in bed.

Slowly my eyes opened. The good news was, my headache was completely gone and from my drunken spell; I was feeling much better.

The bad news was...

"Morning."

The strange voice brought me alert. I sat up, as if lightening had stuck me on the ass. I glanced over, my blood shot eyes narrowed down to see a form in my bed.

Oh fuck.

"Jesus." I hissed out and bolted out of my bed. My jeans were unzipped, but still on for the most part. I was in a white wife beater--I didn't remember putting *that* on.

Fuck, fuck, fuck.

"What? What is it?" The form asked, and she was a very pretty form at that. She looked very similar to one of the girls I had turned into "art" a week or two ago. Shoulder length dark brown hair and grey-blue eyes, with lips to die for. And I'm sure under those covers were two very pert breasts, thighs that could kill, with shapely hips to match. She was gorgeous. And, worst of all, she was *alive*.

"How the fuck did I get here?" I wasn't so fucked up to realize that I was in my own place, my own room. And as I glanced about frantically, nothing I could tell was out of place. I'd spend the rest of Sunday making sure, though.

"You told me the way. I walked you home. You musta' been pretty out of it, Sam."

"Fuck!" I screamed hoarsely, suddenly. She *knew* my Goddamn name!

She sat back against my headboard, looking startled.

"You're acting like some caged tiger," she said with a small nervous smile.

"Maybe because I can't remember shit about last night," I spat out wishing I could handle my alcohol better.

"You did have a lot to drink. Look, I don't want to be a bother, okay? I'll leave. I just didn't…didn't want you to choke on your vomit or anything."

I watched her silently, mulling things over in my mind with a blinding speed. Did she see anything? Don't be silly, all of it is destroyed. What's destroyed? *It*. What? Evidence. The bodies, the pictures, the body parts?

Think rationally, she obviously didn't see a thing because she was acting utterly normal. What if she was covering up? How fucked up does that sound? Shut up. I met her eyes again and then said a bit more calmed down now, "Look, sorry, I just wasn't expecting to see anyone in my bed, I guess."

"Hey, it's cool. It happens to the best of us. If it's all the same, I'll leave." She flashed me a polite, soft grin. I caught that look in her eyes, and those lips… Jesus.

"Yeah, I have to get ready for work." Shock was still clouding much of my rational thinking.

I fucked her? I almost fought back a dry heave. I've never fucked a…a *living* girl before. Oh thank God I was drunk while it happened. And yet…I didn't feel too sick, if anything I felt…

"Great."

I glanced up, seeing her smile again. She had been answering my last response to her. God. I was freaking out. And I had to be at work in about…

The clock read: 9:22 am. About an hour and a half.

"Yeah." I mumbled, watching her get up from

my bed, and start to get dressed. She was beyond perfect, the more I watched...she was so healthy, vibrant, warm, and that smile...whatever had gone down last night, suddenly, I didn't seem to mind any of it. If anything I wanted more. Yes, I wanted more. I licked my lips and headed towards her. I placed my hand over hers as she moved to pull her jeans up. I met her eyes.

"Look, fuck work," I said evenly as she met my gaze. "Stay a bit longer?"

She watched me, reading my expression. My first fuck with a living woman and I couldn't remember it. Now, I would change that, after all, I was getting wet down there and who am I to deny my pussy? Exactly. Besides, not once had she mentioned my extravagantly unique furniture and home décor—so, why not?

"You sure?"

With that I pushed her back onto my bed and then slid on top of her. I felt those nipples push through the shirt she had pulled on. I grabbed a breast roughly and began to grope her shamelessly. And it seemed, no matter how rough I was, she loved it. Perfect...like artwork.

7

5:09 PM

We spent all morning fucking. Most of it hardcore, some soft, whatever we were in the mood for. And the more I fucked her, the more I found that I liked her touch upon my body. She worshipped me, utterly and thoroughly. She begged for my touch, harsh or not, begged for me to cum, she simply begged. A dead girl had never given me this type of rush before, this type of…power. She was art. Everything about her was perfect...this was bad. Very bad.

She left around three-thirty. Since I had already called in sick to work, I used the rest of my day off to clean the hell out of my apartment. I then headed to my freezer and pulled out an eyeless head. The skin of this particular girl had turned a pale blue, with lips ghastly white. The eye sockets at one point had leaked rivers of dark blood and then some clear fluid. Now it was all frozen to the skin like some very disturbing tears.

I thawed the head out and grabbed my tools. I decided to work, to keep my mind off of that girl I had encountered last night and this morning. The sex made me weak, made me feel amazing. I craved it now, like a drug. Not good. What was going on with me? I grabbed a pair of pliers and opened the now thawed out mouth of the head of the girl I was working on. I clasped the metal prongs about the front tooth and wiggled it some.

Wiggle.

Wiggle.

SNAP!

The tooth cracked off, and normally, had she not been frozen, blood would've gushed down, but she was no better than a Popsicle. I sighed, I just…I wasn't deriving as much pleasure from this as I usually did. Soon, the rest of her teeth were extracted (some ripped off with some of her gum lining, but I knew how to clean that off easily. Like I said, Martha Fucking Stewart).

I took my teeth and cleaned them well, bleaching them, scrubbing them, making them as white as possible, which was pretty damn white. Once I had finished I headed back into my bathroom and over to my sink. I rarely used this sink to brush my teeth or wash my hands, since it was under construction. I was remodeling the basin. Instead of a white porcelain basin, it was a basin made out of human teeth, sealed with clear grout. Quite pretty really.

I set to work, adding my teeth to the collection, still trying to get my mind off of the fabulous fuck I had last night. Her name was Ally. Damnit! No names!

And yet, I knew…it was too late. I was smitten, and I knew it. It didn't take a rocket scientist to figure that out.

I mean, honestly now, I understand the system that society has, I know how to play the game. I figured it out at a very early age, in fact. I had a high school chemist teacher who gave an essay for his class final. (I know, I know what the hell does an essay have to do with chemistry? Fuck if I know, but! I had more of a chance to B.S. in writing than I did with the mathematical equations, right?)

So I did that, I B.S.'ed. I bull shitted (or would it be shat?) So I could get my god damned A, my god damned gold star! And it worked. So very easily, I had learned how to manipulate the system and the people about me to my will. Pretty people always get the best of everything—and I'm quite pretty. Successful and intelligent people also get the best of everything; yes I have success and intelligence. Once I learned this? Once I learned just how easy it was to put up one mask to shield the true face—as long as you dotted all of *their* "i's" and *their* "t's"—then I was seen as the golden girl. The woman who could do no wrong—a Virgin Mary, if you will. (What kinda' virgin by the way, craps out a kid? Not a good virgin, that's for sure.)

Learning this trick, learning how to play all of their games and I had grown into a damned good game player. If I had my way, the world would be filled with nothing but the best of everything. Fine wine, fine art, fine culture… None of the riff-raff, none of the stupidity. But, that's just some delusion of grandeur, right? Until then, I find those who see the world as I do, people like Gwenyth Paltrow and… Gwenyth Paltrow, heh, she seems to get what I'm getting at. Kind of.

In fact all of Hollywood seemed to get that...
Entertain the bourgeoisie. Entertain the
masses, entertain any and all who seek entertainment. Gotta past the time in some way,
right? So we've established that I'm good at
what I do, good at living a life full of jump-
ing through hoops with labels galore, but I'm
even BETTER at living a life in which I create
the rules. Me and only me.

So here comes that argument, can an insane
person have feelings? Who knows? I never actually declared myself insane, so don't fucking ask me. I guess the way I'll play this
one out is, whatever gets my pussy wet and my
nipples hard, right? But in truth, I did like
her. A lot.

Knock.

Knock.

Knock.

I stopped, my sink nearly done, same with my
shower. My two prized pieces of work, besides
my 1930's bathtub. I sniffed some and waited-
-did I hear something?

Knock.

Knock.

Yep. I headed over towards my front door
and before I peered out the peephole I called
out, "Who's there?" I guess it's a bit redundant to look, but like I said, obsessive com-
pulsive. And instantly, before I even *looked*
I knew who it was. Ally.

"It's me, Ally."

I cleared my throat and straightened up.
My heart fluttered, doing the ol' one two ac-
robatic tricks in my chest. God, she looked
gorgeous. My throat seemed to dry up and my

palms became sweaty and cold. I slowly opened my door and offered the best Cheshire grin I could.

She had take-out food in her hands and a smile on those lips. I could fuck her right here, in the open front porch of my apartment without thinking twice.

"Hey, what's all this?"

"I brought dinner. I thought maybe you might be hungry from today's lil'…escapades." She sent me a sly grin and I felt my legs turn to rubber. I stepped back allowing her to step inside. Pre art. But I hadn't done any-thing to her...yet.

I showed her to the table, why not? I had finished my sink, well almost. There was noth-ing to hide, and everything was clean, except me. It helped to be a neat freak, believe me. "Hang on, just a sec. I need to wash up real quick."

She nodded her head, setting the food down. Those big innocent eyes of hers gave me shiv-ers up the spine. I went back into my bath-room and readied myself. I cleaned up some and within a matter of minutes, I headed back out, feeling a *slight* bit better about my grungy appearance.

"Wow, you clean up nice," she said through that wicked grin of hers.

I gasped, though I tried to hold it in. In this lighting, she looked like that same girl! The one I saw at the club, replicated a hun-dred times over. The one I had ripped the in-testines out of…

And then she was gone. I blinked, my face ghastly white.

"You okay?" She asked gently.

I blinked. That face was gone and replaced with hers. God, she was beautiful. "Actually, what if we just skipped dinner and went straight to desert?" I put on a smirk, my suaveness hopefully covering up my sudden startle.

"You're the boss."

I could've creamed right then and there.

8

2:52 AM

We remained in my bed together for a long time. Sex once again had been mind blowing, and I was still unsure if my head was connected to my body or not. I knew I was head over heels for this work of art, I mean, girl.

I watched her, lying on her back, bare breasts pointed up. She glanced over to meet my slightly lecherous gaze.

"What are you thinking about?" She asked in that soft feminine voice of hers.

I watched her…so perfect. That body, that hair… but more importantly, those eyes. Those teeth. It would be so easy to take my pillow and just choke her, strangle her until she couldn't breathe anymore. And yet, something stopped me. Something pulled me back. Never, *ever* had I slept with a live woman before. And now that I have and am completely enjoying it? These thoughts plagued me.

And in that small, fleeting second, throughout all my darkness, I felt it. The one chance, the one *stab* I had at normalcy was all right here with this girl, with Ally. All of it was right here. I could start over, well, mentally I could. I wouldn't kill anymore, I could live in perfect peace and happiness with her. It would be like...An artisan's dream.

And yet, those eyes...those teeth, I just needed one more set. It would be so...NO! Not Ally! I decided right then and there, I couldn't be by this girl. Like I said, I may have been a monster, but I had logic, and this time, I needed time to think things over and deal with all of these new...ugh, emotions.

"Nothing," I finally answered, in the darkness, still meeting her eyes. Those perfect eyes.

"Yeah, right," she grinned. I could make that much out. I felt a hand caress my stomach. I moved back as if her touch was poison.

"Are you okay?"

"No. I think it'd be best if you left."

"Right now?"

"Yeah." The truth was, if she stayed, I didn't know what I'd be liable to do.

She didn't even question me--she was such a good girl. God, this Ally...I shook my head. I didn't even want to think about it. She got up and out of my bed and quickly dressed. She moved with a silken speedy grace that flowed like smooth water. And just like that, as soon and as unexpectedly as she had arrived, she was gone.

I sat up in my bed and caught my reflection in my mirror across the way. I looked haggard, in turmoil, tortured. Why and *how* could one girl do this to me? I watched myself for what seemed like hours and then slid out of my bed. I headed into my kitchen to grab a drink.

Pst…

I glanced back at my fridge. I needed to talk, okay? I preferred to talk to myself at about three in the morning than call someone up and wake them.

She could be someone you may actually like…

"You think so?"

Oh completely.

I opened my freezer and spotted the head of the girl I had shoved on the hook the day before. I took it out and placed it gently on the cutting board built into my kitchen counter top. I then grabbed a Snapple from the fridge.

"I just…I don't know what to do."

You like her.

"That's a bold statement."

Not really. If you lie to yourself, who else are you actually going to be honest with?

"That's a good point." I took a sip of my apple flavored Snapple.

So say it, you like her. But, you're confused…

"No shit." I rubbed my lips. "I've never really been in a situation like this before, you know? I just need to think."

I think you should go with what makes you happiest. Do you know what that is?

"Happiness is bullshit. They make pills for it now. Besides I'm 'happy' with my art."

Not really, if you like her and she makes you happy, maybe that's the way to go. Your art will only go so far.

I was silent now. There was no logical flaw in that statement--it was all true. She…Ally made me happy.   I was actually happy!

"I think," I slowly started.   "You're onto something."

Of course I am.

"It's just a matter of taking things one step at a..."

Knock.

Knock.

Oh shit!   I glanced at the head and then moved as quickly as possible.   I shoved it back into the freezer and closed it.   I wiped down the counter with my ready-to-use dish rag and wearily made my way to the door.   I peered out the peephole, though once again, I'm not sure as to why I did.   I knew it was *her*.   It was Ally.

I slowly opened the door. She stepped in and offered me the softest of smiles.

"Sorry I came back, but...I just felt like it'd be completely wrong if I left you right now."

I didn't say anything. I really didn't know what to say.   It was the first time the cat had ripped out my Goddamn tongue.

"I can make you some coffee if you'd like," she offered.

"Uh..."

"Here, I'll do it.   You seem as white as a ghost."   She stepped past me and into the kitchen.   I stood there, thinking, always *thinking*.

I could hear her rummaging about in my kitchen.

"Hey, Ally!" I called out.   But it was too late.

She gasped just as I bolted into my kitchen.

"I didn't know you liked Snapple *so* much!" She looked over her shoulder, her eyes meeting mine. "I would've brought you...are you okay? You look even worse."

"Uh yeah, I'm fine. I thought maybe…never mind." I folded my arms over my chest. Her gasp had been a wake up call. No matter these thoughts and feelings, I still needed to keep my wits about me.

Happiness.

And my happiness. "So…you were worried about me?" I watched her as she moved with that perfect, artful grace around the kitchen—figuring out where this and that was located. The sounds of coffee brewing soothed me some-how.

"I don't want to sound like some obsessed psycho or anything, but..." she laughed gen-tly, and I had to join in, how could I not? "I guess I've just never met anyone like you before." She leaned on my counter top. The shirt she was wearing was pressed against her breasts tightly.

"I'm sure you say that to everyone," I scoffed out.

"Actually..." she answered back with a star-tling silence. "... you're my first."

"Your first?"

"The first woman I've ever…" she trailed off.

I watched her, studied her. My eyes nar-rowed some and I licked my lips. I could feel thoughts of all natures, dark and light flut-tering about my brain like lost butterflies in a windstorm.

"Don't let that throw you," I said quietly and looked down. I couldn't bear to meet her eyes. The things she was saying... it was so...personal. I suppose I did know her on that level. After all, I did fuck her raw. I just was never used to hearing so much from a girl before. I never gave them the time, nor the chance.

"Why not?" Her intuition was steady, I could pick up on it. Perhaps that was what attracted me to her that night in the small café, at least, some of it. Most of it had been my sheer drunkenness.

"Because," I rubbed my lips and then glanced up with a false smile. "How's that coffee coming?"

"Sam." She said now, looking me over. I could tell she wanted to talk. I winced as she used my name, but bit my tongue. I was in a flurry of too many things right now in order to be angered over that. "Look, like I said, you're my first woman and I guess when I saw you that night, inebriated or not, you were still sweet. You reminded me some lost little girl, you know?"

This was going to be deep.

"Well, I mean, someone who is searching for something. So, I took a risk, fuck I take risks all the time, so why not take another one, you know? And it ended up being one of the most…" She paused and brushed some hair away from those gorgeous eyes of hers. "Amazing moments of my life. I didn't realize just how beautiful someone could be. And, well, as I said I really don't want to come off as being fast or strange or anything, but, after spending today with you…God." She laughed gently, it was a laugh of pure mirth. "Anyway, I really enjoyed it, and I enjoy you. And I guess

I wanted to thank you for letting me take that risk with you, and making it one of the best damn things I've ever done."

I was utterly silent now. Those eyes…God, they'd look great in my shower. That smile. Those perfect white teeth lining my sink. I could be one step closer to finishing my projects if I took her. So. Fucking. Close. I shook my head, trying to shake my thoughts out of it. I felt like I was going to cry, scream… kill. "You need to leave," I hissed, standing up abruptly.

She blinked.

"Excuse me?"

"You *need* to go." I clenched my teeth, not looking her in the eye.

"Alright, I'll go. I didn't mean to offend you, I swear. I just had to tell you because…" She stepped forward. "Because I thought you might've felt the same way I did."

"Oh yeah?" I asked so quietly that I didn't recognize my own voice. "And what feeling is that?"

"Happiness," she answered her eyes finally meeting mine.

And it flooded back to me, all of it--the mixed emotions, the differences between need and want. I glanced down, catching my breath in my throat. It was like some sick joke, like someone out there was watching my life on one of those goddamned reality TV shows or something. Except my reality wasn't filled with eating giant Madagascar cockroaches or trying to sing my ass off for some record label deal I'll never really get. My reality was my art first and foremost, then my work, then everything else. Mom, bills, need to conform—all of that was in the back burner.

I knew I wasn't exactly well, ever since I was young. Was it because I had no father to look up to? Maybe because I was a lonely child? Mom never I don't even fucking know. All I know is, here I am, twenty-eight years old, getting as much pleasure as possible as I continue to remain in control over all I create. My pieces of beauty, my sculptures, my décor, all my art. After all, for all the day in and day out crap I have to put up with? All the stupidity and idiocy of this retarded race, I deserve a little fun, a little reward for my own "suffering".

Heh, right.

I could feel it creeping up on me, some rising wave of undeniable heat, some magma rising to the top ready to explode from the volcano. Release. I didn't even realize my hands were shaking until Ally placed hers over mine. I jerked back from such physical contact.

A dead body wouldn't do this.

Then again, a dead body couldn't comfort anything either.

Comfort what? Are you some fucking wimpy pussy? Backing out now?

It's not about that at all, but it sure is nice to--

To what?

"Sam?" She whispered, looking to me now. I guessed my complexion couldn't look too good with all the anguish I was feeling within.

"Really, Ally," I said now through clenched teeth. "Just…just GO!"

And she didn't budge an inch like I had commanded.

Like I had warned.

Then again, it probably would've been impossible for her to move anywhere due to the fact that I had uncontrollably shot my hand out to grip her throat. Her pretty eyes widened like a deer's eyes who had just been caught in some car's headlights.

I slammed her back, the coffee maker was still on, and she crashed into it with my hand locked firmly around her weak, delicate throat. Black, scalding hot coffee spilled all down her lower back, burning the backs of her long soft legs. Oh well, I didn't need those legs right now, anyway. She tried to scream out in pain, but she simply couldn't due to the fact that my hand was locked about her throat like some iron vise.

Her skin was paling, red veins grew like mythical vines in her eyes, and I could feel that pulse rapidly beat for life within her. She was dying, as simple as that. She would've tried to thrash and kick at me all she might but I suspected the coffee had done some real damage, not too mention I wasn't some weakling. I was a pro at this kind of thing.

I felt the warm coffee and bits of glass under my bare feet. The ribbons of pain I felt cut through only geared my rage towards her. I shoved her once, twice, three times back against the counter top hard, her lips turning that infamous pallid blue color. She was losing it fast.

That is, until I let her go.

She fell back against the counter top breathing in strangled gasps. Now her tears would come. A bright pink bruise shaped like my hand print appeared on her fragile throat and

I watched her like some hawk would its unsus-
pecting prey.

Tears fell down those beautiful cheeks now,
though I doubt she was aware of it. I knew the
state of sheer shock she was in. I had seen
so many girls go into it before. It was then
I knelt down, quick as lightening and grabbed
a glass shard from the floor. I stood up and
felt a sharp blow to my stomach from one of
her goddamn knee caps. I coughed, sputtering
out. Now *that* was totally unexpected. She
then darted to get past me, but once again I
really do think that coffee slowed her down a
lot--I caught her. I hooked my arm around her
chest and sliced the glass shard right across
her throat, breaking through her layers of
flesh and muscle, stabbing in with such speed
and force, right past her larynx and into her
very jugular.

She stood there, held in my arms for a moment or two, twitching as her nerves died
slowly. I then dipped down, bringing my lips
over hers and kissed her deeply, sealing off
any chance at air she might've had in her last
moments. Blood now spurted out wildly, the
artery pumped--trying to keep her alive, but
that precious life giving liquid was wasted as
it was shot out. More bright red blood spewed
out down her throat, neck, some even splashed
up onto her cheeks and then dripped down, mixing and intertwining with her tears. A thin
film of mucus ran down her nose, dripping from
her chin. She was whiter than a ghost, and
the streaming blood seemed to contrast her
color beautifully. Art. She was art.

So there. That's my happiness. Art. Art
makes me happy. And she is my artwork. They

all are.   With the rest of her parts I can
finish my remodeling.   I collect, chose, gathered, and put together.   I was the creator.
Fuck you if you read into it anymore than it
ought to be.   After all, like I said, I have
logic right?   I'm no better than any other human being, person, so why do I do what I can?
Because like any other person could choose to
say, I can.
   I can.

9

6:01 AM

Life goes on, you know? At least, mine does. I kept things at my place silent for a few months. And you bet your top dollar that was harder than HELL! Usually I splurge on my birthday—really go gung ho with a girl, but not this time. I had to celebrate being twenty-nine with a Gwenyth flick and apple sorbet.

The media and trusty police force were now looking for a few of my girls. It's tricky to dispose of the bodies. I stripped them all down as much as I could, scraping off all fat, muscle, tendons, and everything else with some handy house hold tools like: razors, jig saws, wood files, chisels, and some cooking utensils like: a strainer, an ice pick, or, of course, a butcher knife. Sure this work was messy and tedious, but I could not have that sort of evidence, not to mention *smell* and *filth* in my apartment. I used my bathroom usually—all the tile on the floor made mopping up the blood so simple, just add some bleach and hell, a spoon full of sugar, and I was good to go. Beat that, Mary Poppins.

If I wanted to shake things up a bit, I'd use my kitchen—that metal dining table worked wonders. Steel reflects everything allowing me to watch myself peel off the flesh bit by bit. It was hard not to get turned on during such frivolous activities—but I can handle myself. Once I had all the flesh off to the best of my ability (and oh yes, I'm a perfectionist as I've mentioned countless times before) I collected it all in trash bags and set it out to the trash compactor to be burned.

Still, never-the-less, it was redundant work.

Thank god for Gwenyth's movies. They serve as a good background noise in order to help keep me focused. She's so determined and so stunning. So proper and detached from society—yet she rules the sheep that is the public under her thumb. She is amazing—though I really wish she would lay off the Jimmy Choo pumps. They're really cliché.

Once the bones are stripped clean, I bleach them in my 1930s tub until they are white as a ghost, then coat them in the enamel I've taken from my work (after all, everyone has perks at their jobs, right?) and I use them as the arms and legs of my home furniture. Sure I have to double up some of them because one little piece of spinal vertebrae won't cover the weight of the sofa couch that I created to go on top, but once I place them as the literal legs of the couch, chair, whatever—they serve their purpose. My chairs are made out of bones, mixed with some steel piping, as well as cushions to go on top. My entertainment stand, my lamp fixtures—all creations of the brilliance that is me… A place for everything and everything in its place.

I decorated tastefully enough to blend in such art with what is normally bland furniture—so much so, that if I ever did have company, they never really noticed until they looked. But, a simple answer like, *Oh, I got this specially ordered from Switzerland from that one industrial artist who did the alien in the movie,* Alien, *H.R. Giger? Yeah, him.*

Con is obviously in the word confidence and if you act confident about anything? Then people, the sheep that they are, believe anything. I've more than mastered this trick.

Monday morning. God, that alarm buzzed off loudly beside my ear, letting me know it was time to get up and "bring home the bacon." Sighing, I sat up, rubbing my eyes groggily, another day, another dollar. I hit the button and slipped out of my bed. Once I was up, I spent the next five minutes perfecting my bed, making it, tucking sheets in, giving my bed "hospital" corners.

There, perfect.

Did I mention I'm a bit anal retentive when it comes to cleanliness and keeping things neat and tidy? Well, I am. Soon I was in the shower, my now *finished* shower--thanks to…what was her name? Annie? Alba?

A drip of soap from my conditioner splashed into my eye.

"FUCK!" I rubbed it out, the burning stung like no other. It felt like a red hot poker was taken from its resting place in stoked fire and then shoved, rammed right into my eye socket. Ally! That was it! I finished, already I was feeling a bit pissy. Soap in the eye really didn't help my mood much.

My shower, however, looked wonderful. The clear, plexi glass bricks looked lovely--all the eyes fixed into place, as if trying to look at the very meaning of life itself.

The only meaning they'd find would be my nude, clean body.

Soon I dressed for work, my attire respectable, dressy as always, (though not overly done) modern, chic, and just that slight hint of sexiness to get all the looks I'd like, but still remain in utter control.

Clad in a pair of black silken slacks and a black blouse with a white large collared shirt beneath, giving my blouse white cuffs and a white collar, I headed into my kitchen. I popped my fridge open and grabbed a Snapple along with an apple, morning breakfast, and then was on my way to work. I was in my car and very much stuck in fucking city traffic. Oh, the joys of urban living in Madison, Wisconsin.

Everyone is a fucking "cheesehead" here. All the houses look the same, all the buildings covered in dust, and though they do have a city—it's pathetic.

The only reason why I ever came to this state was because no one else wanted to. I could do my art here. I mean seriously who wants to be out in the middle of flat prairie land nowhere? The ones who want to meet me, heh, that's who.

I simply found a good job I could put my degree to, got hired on, and viola! I have luxurious condo in butt-fuck nowhere, in a "podunk" city that barely exists on a map. Who the hell cares about what's happening in

Madison, Wisconsin when there's so much going on in New York, Or Los Angeles?

Still, I couldn't push back those thoughts that I had been attaining over every god-damn girl I saw. Even if I was in a hick city, I still needed to keep my cool and not get sloppy. Right now things were a little tighter than normal. Speaking of tight... I just wanted to take her, slam her into a wall, crush her little fragile throat, feel her muscles contract and hear those little sobs of fear. I wanted to see the hook protrude right through her abdomen as I hung her like wet laundry above my pride and joy 1930's bathtub--no wait! I wanted to see the blood spill as I used my delicious hook to ram it into her hot, tight little cunt and rip it all the way up to her fucking mouth. Slit from the clit.

Just then someone honked. God DAMMIT! As if my morning hadn't started off shitty enough, I have some asshole honking at me. I gritted my teeth and then screeched off through the intersection at my green light. So what if I didn't instantly drive forward the second my light turned green? It's been nine months, fucker. NINE fucking MONTHS! I fucking hate humanity and their stupid little ways.

But, I could wait. I could indeed wait until I collected another one of my girls. With the fucking pig cops combing the area, searching for what they'd never find, I could hold off. I would never be caught, ever. I'm not like the others...Dahmer, Gacy, Bundy...no I'm much different--they were caught. I however, will never be caught, never be suspected. I've got the perfect disguise... I'm a female.

Besides, the leftover remains of my girls

will never ever be found. And even if they are? There's nothing to tie them back to me. I'm too careful. I hate it when our trash burning service in these damn apartments stops due to too much pollution. That's bullshit. Alice, or Abba--no, her name was Ally, I couldn't exactly burn her to black nothingness. That stupid rule was in effect when I had so conveniently wanted to dispose of her body (I kept it a bit longer than I meant to, I wanted one last amazing fuck with the bitch in the end) But, like I said, I had other ways. I'm careful, perfect in every way, and very aware. Still… nine damn months had gone by. I could do this.

10

8:00 AM

"Morning."

"Morning."

"Good morning!"

"Yeah."

"Hey! Good--"

"Morning! Yeah, yeah…" I briskly cut off whatever fuckwad had said "morning" to me for the thousandth time and slunk into my cubicle. I sat down at my desk (in which, my cubicle did hold a very lovely view of the downtown city) and clicked my computer on. I didn't want to have to deal with any co-workers, any gossip, any stupid office chat, or anything *human* for that matter. I just wanted to work, take my mind off of what I *really* wanted to do…

"Hey, Samantha?" came a rather bland voice from behind me. I fought the urge to shiver. It was one thing to use my name, *Sam*, but it was another thing entirely to use my full name, Samantha. I've never cared for names, though of course if mine must be used, i.e. work, mom, etc. then so be it. But using my *full* name? That irks the hell out of me.

I spun about in my nicely upgraded swivel

chair. I had the chair that the entire office would fight over--ha ha. I looked to the boring, dull man at the opening of my cubicle, wearing some boring brown suit, with a rather boring toupee on his boring head. Roger Miller. This man had had a crush on me ever since I started working as the top interior design consultant here, five years ago. I loathed him. It was hard not to fall asleep while listening to him talk and the fact that he used my full name? Die.

"Yes?" I answered as sweetly as possible, pulling a fake grin upon my red lips. Such a good actress, give the girl an Oscar.

"You okay?" he asked in his rather dull way. I could feel my eyelids drooping already.

"I have a bit of a headache," I lied.

"Oh… well, would you like some aspirin?" My eyes slid to his toupee… didn't he know how *bad* it looked?! Like some rat just decided to crawl up onto his skull and then just *die* there?

"Naw, it's okay really." I flashed another cursory grin and then arched a dark brow, my entire body language telling him to leave. And leave *now*.

"Okay. There's some coffee in the lounge, y' know…"

"Yeah, maybe I'll get some when I feel a bit more up to it. I think I've just got a case of the 'Mondays' or something."

"Knock, knock!" sang the perkiest bitch I'd ever met. Susan Wells--her bleached blonde head stuck its way into the opening of my cubicle. Perfectly white teeth smiled largely against a falsely tanned face. "Did I hear someone say that they had a case of the 'Mondays' in here?" I hated that perky bitch.

"Yeah." What the FUCK is this?! "Everyone Come and Bother Sam Day" today? Once again I fought back from gritting my teeth and instead kept a warm grin on my lips.

"Aww! Well, I heard that Tori brought in doughnuts! They're in the lounge. There's some scrumpity dumpity coffee in there too, Sam."

Scrumpidty dumpity? I couldn't help but repeat silently--she made me sick in ways I didn't know the human body could be repulsed. Everything about that overly tan, bleached blonde twig was fake. Right down to her silicon breasts, and bo-tox injected face.

"Maybe I'll grab some in a bit. I'm not too hungry right now," I said, faking a wince to show my so-called headache.

"Let me guess, you already had your morning apple, huh?" Susan asked, faking a personality.

"Yep." I swear I was starting to get a real headache now. I stared at Susan's bleached blonde hair, not a strand out of place, every bit of was so affixed with what seemed like four quarts of hairspray. I could smell the hair care products from where I sat and wanted to vomit.

"Oh Sam!" she giggled. My stomach lurched.

Roger seemed a bit left out of the conversation by now. Like I said, dull. I almost forgot he was still there, actually. He shifted a bit uneasily and then said, "I have some aspirin in my desk if..."

"I'm fine, really." I said rather curtly. He looked as if he were some six-year-old boy who just had his little puppy dog run down brutally by some asshole motorist.

I wanted to be that asshole motorist.

"Well, the doughnuts are just de-LIGHT-ful..." Susan chimed in.

I got up, my four inch stiletto high heels clicked dully on the dark blue carpet of the office. I walked over to Roger and snatched that God-awful toupee off his boring head, shoved it with sheer force right past those frighteningly white teeth of Susan and down her throat, knocking a few teeth out in the process. Blood spurted out from her mouth as she began to gag on the hair piece, choking. I watched as her horribly tan skin (or maybe she wasn't tan. Maybe she had jaundice? Any-way...) turned that all too familiar pale blue. Although, when you mix blue and yellow togeth-er, Susan looked a bit green as well.

I then turned to Roger and grabbed his bland shoulders tightly. I brought my knee up, slam-ming straight in the balls, making him double over in severe, throbbing pain. The kind of pain, I've been told, that makes you sick to your stomach whenever a guy gets slammed in the balls. And as my knee remained up, I reached over and grabbed the spiked pump from my foot and then slammed that heel right into his mundane eye socket. His dull brown eye popped as the heel shoved into it, blood spurting out everywhere. Eyeball fluid dripped down his chin.

"SHUT UP!!!" I screamed out at the now two dead corpses before me.

Yeah right...think I'm that stupid? I'm not dumb enough to actually act out a fantasy like that in such a populated environment. Like I said, I'm sick, but not an idiot. I *wanted* to do those things, but instead, I pulled on my award winning grin and nodded as Susan spoke on and on… and then I finally said, while she paused for a breath, "I'll go grab some coffee in a bit. I gotta get my analysis typed right now though. Mr. Stanley wants it on his desk by 9:30."

"Oh, gotcha' girly," Susan grinned and then winked. Jesus H. CHRIST, the bitch wore fake eye lashes too. I really felt like I was going to be sick. My grey eye twitched some now. Susan then headed off, leaving me with Mr. Boring. Couldn't the man take a hint?

"Well, I'll uh…see you around, Samantha?" he then asked gently.

"Possibly," I snapped, then spun back to face my computer, thinking that would give him a hint. His shadow left my cubicle's area as he then left, giving me my privacy. I hated humans, and I loathed predictable human behavior.

I logged onto my computer and pulled up the Richtor File. I opened it and began looking over blue prints and plans to this man's string of dance clubs all throughout the tristate area. He was a pretty important client, a very wealthy one, who had specifically asked for me to look over his décor since he knew of my fame and expertise. You had to be living under a rock if you didn't know who I was--I was the entire artistic world, co-workers and my boss alike knew it.

That's why I had the only cubicle with the spectacular view of point two skyscrapers and the rest being barren flat lands. Nice. I twisted in my chair some, reading over what had been initially planned--changing a few color schemes here, adding some monochromatics there, giving a few things some flare. The retro look was in style, but it held now a very modern tone with it as well. People seemed to want a vintage décor with a modern twist—way to clash, right?

Soon I heard a soft knock on my cubicle's grey side wall. I didn't even glance over my shoulder. "What?"

"Ms. Ellis?"

"Don't do that."

"Uhm...do what?"

"Accentuate the "L's" in my last name. I *hate* it when people do that."

"Oh, sorry Ms. Ellis," the voice was softer now. I felt a chill go down my spine. What is up with this? First my full name is used by some dull dimwit, and now my last name? I could scream. Nine months, it had been nine months...calm down, Sam. It's okay, just calm it down.

"Yes?" I answered sweetly, still not looking up. I was in the midst of typing up my analysis on the ground plans for the Richtor File. Could these fuckers not see that a genius was at work? Jesus.

"I uh...just wanted to let you know that you have some mail here." That voice responded. It sounded so soft, meek, timid. So...girly... feminine.

I sucked in a deep breath and spun about on my much envied swivel chair and caught sight of the girl talking to me. The supple pink lips seemed so unsure of their words, full breasts barely buttoned down by the dress code of the button up blouse, and rounded hips encased in a navy blue business skirt. Curvy, perfect legs were complimented by spiked heels, and her little tummy seemed to pout out only slightly, making the buttons on that blouse strain a bit.

I could see those green eyes of hers sitting nicely in a jar. Intestines hanging out of her belly like she was some human yo-yo. Her chest split wide open, like a cadaver ready for some scientific explanation, blood oozing everywhere, bits of muscle and fat hanging from her like a freakishly decorated Christmas tree. Perfect. Except for the color of nail polish on those damn finger nails.

"Mail, huh?" My rude demeanor melted away, replaced by a warm and gentle sense every woman has. Only mine was acted out. Where the fuck is my Oscar? "What is it?"

"Uh, it has to do with something about your evaluation on the Johnson File." She answered softly, those full pink lips working over every word as if it was some new toy she was trying out. Her red hair was pulled back in a loose bun, save a few strands about her smooth, beautiful face.

"You *must* be new."

A faint blush crept over her cheeks. "W-why do you say that?"

Oh, she was too perfect! Why am I being tempted?! WHY?!

Ninemonthsninemonthsninemonthsninemonths in my head like a mantra.

"Well, because usually interns who've been here for a while don't read other people's mail. They just deliver it."

Her faint blush grew into full blown crimson now.

"Plus," I added on, not wanting to offend her. Oh no, I wanted her to like me, like me a lot, actually. "I haven't seen you around." I grinned gently.

She let out a small laugh and then shifted some, still a bit uncomfortable. "Yeah. I've… I've uh heard a lot about you, Ms. Ellis."

Those "L's" were soft, I noted.

"Please, call me Sam," I said casually enough.

She nodded. "I just really admire your work. I had to study your style as part of my mid-term. Well we had a chance to pick who it was we would focus on for our project. I picked you."

I knew my head had to have been growing to astronomical proportions, but I loved being worshiped over. After all, I deserved it, right? "You just get out of school?"

"Yes. I mean no. I mean, I'm graduating in a month. I'm Lisa Thatcher." She stuck out her hand to shake mine, and in doing so, dropped all the mail. Quickly she scrabbled down to re-collect it all, giving me the perfect view down her succulent, soft, full—and quite symmetrical breasts.

Breasts that would look so much better sliced right off. Nipples affixed to lamp shades…breasts ripped off with my good ol' trusty hooks. I shook my head and then moved down, helping to pick up some of the mail she had so clumsily dropped.

"Ohmygosh!" She breathed out. "I'm so sorry, I'm just…" She sat up, looking at me. "I'm nervous. It's my first day here and when I found out I was hired at the same place Samantha Ellis..."

I fought off a wince.

"...I mean, that you worked at, I was in total shock. After having gotten a chance to delve into your fashion style, your eye for contrast and those focal points you come up with? Yeah. Especially the way you mesh the vintage look with a more modern motif—keeping things steely, industrial-like almost? Yet, being able to capture the feel of the '30s sort of time period, keeping that humanity intergraded?—that really spoke to me as a designer. No one else these days seems to have such a unique fashion sense as you do."

I grinned. Perfect. "Well, thank you. But I, like you, started out as an intern...and worked my way up. I'm no different than anyone else."

She nodded, her face showing that she took everything I said to heart. It was then I knew that I wanted her--and I knew she would be mine.

Lisa tucked a few strands of crimson hair behind her ears and then stood back up. I followed her, getting another long look at those shapely legs like perfect sculpture. She then handed me my own piece of mail. "Thanks Ms... I mean, Sam. It's tough work, huh? Doing what you do? Being so needed in this interior design community?"

"Naw." I answered, flashing the devil's own grin. "If you love what you do, hard work is like icing on the cake. You gotta' be willing to get a little dirty, get up to your elbows in it, y'know?"

She nodded emphatically.

And I knew I should've stopped myself right there--but come on! This girl was hanging on

my every word for fuck's sake! I had to continue. I would be careful. Very careful. I
always was. "You know, I could show you some
more of my stuff sometime, kinda' show you the
ropes, the tricks of the trade and all that
jazz. Maybe give you some tips on the "do's
and don'ts" of the industry. If you'd like,
that is…"

Bite the bait, bitch.

Her green eyes lit up like the fireworks on
the Fourth of July and she grinned broadly like
some little school girl. I could've sworn she
was going to jump up down cheerleader style,
but she refrained. She tried to calm herself
down, though it was a bit too late. "You really mean it? That would be amazing."

"Sure thing, Lisa. I'm always up for helping out bright go-getters such as yourself."

Lisa's smile I thought would split her head
in half for the size that it was now. "Okay!"
She was as flushed as ever, and Jesus, I wanted
her.

"How about Friday after work? I'll be busy
all day, but maybe I can show you some of my
floor plans and have some dinner or something
that night?" Completely casual, completely
friendly. I knew how to play the game so damn
well.

"Friday…" She paused for a moment and then
looked as if her heart shattered. God, her
emotions played beautifully over that lovely
face. She was such a *girl*. My girl. "I
can't." She looked seriously troubled now.
"I've got a date with my boyfriend."

"Ah, I can understand." The *fucker*. "Saturday night then?"

Lisa thought for a moment and then that

girly, femme smile returned. "Okay. Saturday!"

"Alright, I'll plan on it."

"Do you need my number or anything to get a hold of me?"

"I'll get it through Mr. Stanley--I don't wanna' seem *too* un-professional in front of you on your first day." I winked playfully.

She laughed. I was going to cream myself silly right then and there.

"Right, Sam."

"I'll see you later, Lisa."

She nodded and then turned to head out.

"Oh, and Lisa?" I called out, watching her every move.

"Yes?"

"Try not to read anyone else's mail. That's the first bit of advice I can give you right now." I flashed her a charming, mischievous grin. "Unless it seems really juicy."

She blushed a bit more and smiled timidly back at me, then headed on her merry way.

I felt like a million fucking bucks. I headed out of my cubicle and into the lounge. I'll take some of that coffee now.

As I entered into the briskly air-conditioned lounge I tried not to notice the amounts of dust accumulating against the corners of the walls. The janitors in this building were horrendous. Apparently I had stepped into the lounge during a rather serious discussion--perhaps debate.

"I think it's a hoax."

"A *hoax* John? There are eight missing women! Eight! No relation to one another, all within the same age and all have similar physical descriptions. Why would they just all get together and go, "Hey, we look similar, and we're all about the same age. Let's go and run off and see if anyone notices? That's ridiculous."

"Exactly. There're no bodies that have turned up, right? Nothing to suggest they've been murdered."

"What about that body they found about a year ago? That Christina girl? She was missing for a long time, and then when they found her, she was all cut up, and her eyes and teeth were gone. She was practically just a skeleton. She had been missing for a *long* time. She fits the description of these other girls as well."

"Anna's right. They took forever to identify her because she didn't even her teeth, John. No teeth."

"Oh God. Figures the two women in the room would be on the same side."

"Oh, you're an egotistical bastard!" Diane now huffed out and sipped her coffee.

Anna glared at John and looked back over at the paper.

John noticed me now slip into the lounge and asked me, "What about you, Sam? You gonna' team up with them?"

I smirked, covering up the gritting of my teeth over my name and then headed over to the coffee pot. I pulled a Styrofoam cup up from the stack, one from the middle--I knew it was clean because no one's grimy hands had touched it yet. I poured a cup of coffee and looked to John. "What's the heated debate over?" I knew perfectly well. And that Christina girl? I didn't have time to harvest her bones like I normally would—my work schedule was too hectic that week. Such a good waste, and once I do get rid of my girls? I never return to where I bury them—I know how to play it safe.

"Well, there are eight women missing and Diane and Anna think it's because there's some sick fuck on the loose. I think it's coincidental, maybe a hoax, or maybe they're all a part of some cult. There's just not enough evidence to support their argument." He jutted his thumb over to an enraged Diane and a sullen Anna.

"Hmmm. Well, I can see both sides," I said indifferently. "But, I mean, if you think about it like this, if it was some sort of elaborate hoax, more girls would turn up to be missing, rather than just eight. Eight's a number to cause some concern, but not enough to go, "Okay, there's something fishy goin' on here, you know?"

Diane gave me a thankful smile, and John a satisfied smirk.

"But!" I continued, "If there is some sicko going around and taking these women, then it's likely these women will never be seen again. Odds are they've been killed and disposed of *so* well that the bodies will never be recovered. Quite a brilliantly done crime, just looking at the spectrum of things."

All three were looking at me silently now. God, didn't they have a sense of humor? Assholes.

"I mean," I said evenly, "If they were murdered that is, then it wouldn't make sense to tie them into that other girl Anna brought up. More bodies would've been found, and eventually theirs would turn up in the same fashion-

-more clues would be evident. A psycho killer has to make mistakes simply because they're insane. So, I guess… the best I can do about the whole ordeal is just keep up to date with news and see what unfolds."

"I like the way you think, Sam." Anna looked at me with admiration twinkling in her eye, "Always outside of the box."

Diane simply nodded. Well fuck her. Go on bitch, try and take me on.

"I still think it's a hoax," John added stubbornly.

"Oh John, go suck yourself," Diane sneered.

John flashed her a grin and then reached for a doughnut on the table. I sipped my coffee. Ah, just another normal Monday--and already, I couldn't *wait* for Saturday.

11

4:52 PM

I tapped a few keys on my computer, finishing up my analysis on the Richtor File. Everything looked perfect, beautiful. I was sure Mr. Stanley, my head boss whom I only answer to--though really, he answers to me--I run his fucking company and the sack of pussy shit knows that damn well--would approve. I could sense a small business trip coming up. I didn't just work behind a desk--fuck no. If I did, I'd go insane. Not only did I get to send my artistic opinions out to people on how to decorate their living spaces, bars, clubs, facilities of luxury and convenience, but I oversaw it all, met them in person, and even constructed a few projects. I'm pretty good with my hands, if you haven't noticed already.

I sent the file over to Mr. Stanley's invoice carrier and leaned back in a feline stretch. I felt the smallest vertebral pops in my back that drained me and made me giddy, tired, and ecstatic all at once. When times like this hit, I needed to go to the gym.

"Samantha?"

I held off the gritting of the teeth. With a new girl in my near future, nothing could get me down.

I spun around to see that Roger's toupee was adjusted horribly. God, what a freak. "Yes?"

"How's that headache comin'?" His bland brown eyes conveyed genuine concern, if he only knew...

I feigned a reciprocal authenticity. "All gone now, Roger."

"Okay," he said, slightly nervous. I had that affect on men. "I was wondering if you weren't too busy if...on Friday night that is… if you wanted to y'know…" He paused, a small sweat breaking out above his upper lip.

He had asked me out several times in the past and each and every time I refused. Why did he get so nervous before he asked each time? Didn't he know that the outcome would never, ever change?

"I'm really busy, Roger. I have a few files I'm working on and I can't. Besides, I've told you about how I feel about dating co-workers. I like to keep business and personal lives separate. I'm sure an old pro like you can understand that." Besides, I just remembered that Gwenyth's *E! True Hollywood Story* was on tonight--good thing Lisa and I were meeting on Saturday night instead.

He nodded his head slowly. I was ready to set up a bet, ten bucks that one more nod would knock that damn disgusting piece right off his skull. It stayed. Fuck. "Okay, yeah, I know I was just y'know seeing if..."

"Thanks anyway, Roger." I glanced at the

clock beside my computer. Five o'clock, closing time. "I've gotta' run. You have a nice one, okay?" Another false smile as false as Susan's boobs were.

I watched him and as he moved down the hall and, sure enough, the toupee slid off.

Score!

He knelt and quickly picked it up, hoping no one saw the embarrassing loss. I was sure people did, but it was "proper office etiquette" to act like they didn't. Oh you bet those plastic people would be right beside the water cooler or in the bathrooms, when they found the time, talking about it as though it was bigger than God himself taking a shit. We were all well-mannered...within the confines of the office cubicles at least. Outside... that was a different story. Behind closed doors people have a tendency to become some else entirely, I told myself as I logged off my computer then straightened my desk, making sure things were in their prim and proper place. I'm no different than every other sick fuck running around pretending to be normal... right?

Running on the treadmill at the gym helped put that question out of my mind. I was really starting to feel that good burn and ache stretching myself to the limit-then the news broadcast aired on those hanging TVs--my steps slowed down, and my heart rate went up. Another two bodies had just been discovered about twenty miles away from where that "Christina" girl had been found. It must've been Ally's. The other was from some girl I had taken a long while back. She was anonymous to me now--I only knew that she was mine. But how was

I to tell without them showing the bodies on the news, right?

The bitch was coming back to haunt me. I slowed to a stop on my treadmill and watched as authorities classified the two bodies to have been, "marked with the same aggressive brutalities". I froze, but the treadmill wouldn't let me stop moving. It was suddenly hard to get my limbs to work, how ironic to be in my self-spurned rigor mortis. Two more were found? I listened intently now to the talking idiots on TV reporting on what would either quite possibly make or break me.

"... Still forensic evidence is showing little to no suspect for these gruesome murders. Detective Clairmont of the Madison City Police Department concluded that this is the work of a serial killer. And no further statements were being made at this time."

I breathed in deeply and slumped over the machine. If forensics couldn't find a trace of anything that led back to me, I was in the clear.

"Good workout, huh?" the girl said next to me. A smirk spread over my lips, oh yes, I couldn't *wait* for Saturday night. *Serial killer* my ass...

"Sam," A hand touched my shoulder, my muscles tensed. It was one of my so-called workout buddies, Janine McDormand, too rail thin for my liking, one green eye, the other blue. Mis-matched eyes--utterly disgusting. She must've just arrived after me, and by the way, she was no art project, just another normal freak of nature.

"Yeah?" I answered sweetly.

"Isn't it awful?" she said with one of those

soccer mom pouts (you the look they get when their kid has just totally missed kicking the ball, thus fucking up their team's chance to win. Aw, poor baby.)

Oh she was so serious, so perturbed that her little utopian city wasn't exactly as sweet and happy as she would've liked to think. I had to fuck with her, I mean you gotta take advantage of a win when you get one, right? This was a win.

"Completely. I was really working up a good sweat to that new music video when they switched to news. That's just so rude."

"Not what I meant Sam," she huffed. "I mean the murders. It's scary. I mean, you and I walk alone out to that parking garage all the time!"

She was right. It was scary—they could've found evidence leading back to my apartment! But they didn't, the fuckers. Told you I was careful. If ever I secreted any bodily fluids on my girls--they were burned, and if that didn't work, they were bleached. It paid to be a clean freak. Now she was watching me with those lopsided, mis-matched doe eyes. Here we go.

"Janine, think logically," I got back onto my treadmill. "We're *obviously* not the type."

"What do you mean?"

"Have you seen the *size* of those girls?"

Janine glanced back at the TV screen showing the pictures of the missing voluptuous eight girls complete with a phone number for concerned citizens to call with information—in case anyone gave a shit.

Janine frowned, "It's still sad," climbing onto the empty treadmill next to mine.

Sad, why? Like people don't die everyday? Like somebody else wasn't going to kill them if I didn't? Then I noticed she placed her speed setting up three times higher than usual. I couldn't help but smirk.

12

7:47 PM

I walked into my wonderfully clean apartment to hear the phone ringing. I set my duffle bags down (I keep three in my car, one with my gym clothes, the other with my work clothes, then there's the one with my clubbing clothes).

"Hello?"

"Sam, honey."

My mother.

"Hey mom," I said sweetly. I leaned on my granite kitchen countertop, and tried to reach a Snapple without pulling the phone out of the wall. Having a vintage style came at a small price—but limited mobility on the telephone was worth looking fabulous for. "How's it going?"

"Well, honestly, I'm a bit worried, you know."

"Why? What's going on?"

"Haven't you been listening to the news?"

"Oh, yeah."

"'Oh yeah'?! Sam! I don't want my daughter living in a city like that."

"Madison, Mom? Madison, Wisconsin home of the "cheeseheads"? You're in New York, somehow I think that might classify as a little bit more dangerous."

"Well, New York doesn't have some sick freak going around a murdering young girls."

"You heard about that too? It's made national news?"

"Well, no… But, I read the papers and the small side articles. I like to know what's going on in the city you're living in. I'm a mother, Sam. I care about you and your life. It really bothers me that you're living in a place that's so dangerous."

"Mom… Did you just hear what you said?"

"Well, okay, so New York can be a little harsh. Still…"

"You were mugged in broad daylight—two cops watched from the Dunkin' Donuts."

"It wasn't BROAD daylight. It was… cloudy. And those cops were after that prick in a second."

"You just a have a thing for guys in uniform, huh?"

"Ha! Seriously though, sweetie, I hate having to worry about you."

"Mom, I'm fine, okay? Besides everything they found dealing with any of that serial killer crap is a good twenty miles or more away from me."

"Still Sam, it doesn't make me feel much better. I'd feel safer if you had a nice young man to stay there with you."

Ah ha, I knew there was more to this phone call than met the ear. "Mom…" I futilely protested.

"I'm just saying, Sam. There're many men

out there who'd love to date you."

"I'm picky mom, what can I say?"

"Picky? Or lesbian?"

I fought the urge to scream at her now. "Mom, we've been over this many times. I'm not queer, okay? I just need to find Mr. Right, that's all. Besides, with all that's going on, Mr. Right could be Mr. Gouge Out My *Right* Eye Ball."

"That's not funny, Sam," My mom sighed. "I guess I just want some grandkids, you know? Could you do that for your mother?"

I fought back the sudden need to purge everything I had consumed that day. I *hated* children. Hated them. "Yeah, I know mom. You've been after me to have kids ever since what now? Since I was like seven?"

Mom laughed. "Sam, you make me sound obsessed."

"I'm just going by what I hear." I headed to my fridge and pulled out a Snapple, then opened it. "So besides worrying over me every single second, how've you been?"

"Good. I've…" And my mom went off to list the boring, doldrums of her life. She was seeing this new man, complained about how her manicurist chipped her pinky nail, talked about a sale that was going on at Nordstrom's.

"Uh-huh. Right. Oh yeah, you'd have to complain, naturally…" I muttered, not really paying attention. I had opened my freezer and inside were a few...things wrapped up tightly in saran wrap. I removed two of those things and placed them gingerly on my counter top. I knelt down.

"Sam?"

"Hm?"

"I said, what did you think?"

"Well…" Shit. Could Alex Trebek repeat the question for 500 please? I took a stab in the dark, "Well, he seems like a nice guy so far, mom."

"You think so?"

Bingo. Damn I'm good. I pulled out a medium-sized cutting board, stood and placed it on the counter top. I then placed the two saran wrapped packages on the cutting and began to unwrap the first frozen package.

"Yeah. What's he look like?"

"Well he has the most entrancing blue eyes, Sam. It makes me get all flustered just when I look at them."

"Mom…" I began.

"Just shut up and listen to your mother, I've been dying to tell this to someone."

"Why don't you tell Millie? She's like your best friend, isn't she?" I really had no need to hear any descriptions of what got my own mother's wrinkled vagina wet or not.

"She's on that cruise in Florida I *just* told you about."

"Oh."

"Look, if you're not going to listen..."

"I'm sorry, I'm just…getting ready to make dinner."

"Oh? What're you having?"

I glanced down at the now two unwrapped packages on the cutting board. They were a pair of mismatched breasts. One I had sliced off a long time ago, I don't recall whose. I could see blue veins snake their way up along to the tip of the blue, pert little nipple. The fat from the breast had been held in place by the saran, and now it was stiff. It looked like frozen Jell-O, though more filmy, and the color yellow it maintained reminded me of custard.

"Breast and custard for desert." I replied vaguely, looking over the severed boob in front of me. Well, that certainly gave new meaning to the expression *Colder than a witch's tit.* I laughed silently at that.

"Chicken breast--white meat only right? If I know you like I do," my mom said jovially over the phone.

"None other, mom," The veins on the other one were thicker and the flesh from where I had chopped it off was all swollen, a puffy pinkish blue color. A few purplish thin, stringy veins hung from the severed end, dried blood remained. I must have gotten too busy to clean this one off, or something. This nipple was bigger than the other one. There were bite marks all over it--I must've gotten carried away with this girl. Seeing the various puncture marks made me smile nostalgically.

Ah yes, I remembered now! The college graduate I had met at the movie theatres. We had the whole "eye contact" thing going on through the movie then afterwards, I invited her out for drinks, and she accepted. We talked, had a great night out at this small bistro, and the chemistry just really clicked. I then offered her a night cap at my place and as she sat on my couch, while I was supposedly making her drink, I took the axe I held in my guest bedroom's closet, aimed at her head and with one strong swipe, I was able to cleanly take off just the top portion of her skull, making it fly across the room. Her brain was exposed and the blood seemed to have some sort of delayed reaction. It was then, when she cast her beautiful eyes up and noticed her brain starting to slowly leak down her face, did she finally open her mouth to scream.

But, I was prepared. I mean, my walls were pretty thick--but still, someone could have potentially heard her scream, so I had to be ready. I took the gag I had been holding in my back pocket and strapped it about her mouth--it was still opened wide. I then quickly grabbed my handcuffs I also had on me (like I said, I'm always prepared) and cuffed her hands quickly behind her back. She was slow. I mean, for God's sake, she was missing the top of her head. I then took a screw driver that I had also carried in my back pocket and began to delicately wiggle it into her bare brain.

First her eyes did this weird cross-eyed thing that made me laugh--it was funny to watch, then she seized and got this dopey look on her face. I, however, was busy looking at her brain, reminded of spaghetti, when the idea struck me to grab a fork and see if I could pull out her brain like a wet noodle. It was worth a shot, right?

I grabbed a fork from my kitchen and stuck it her skull. As if getting ready to eat a delicious Italian meal and pulled out a strand of her brain, which almost seemed to liquefy on my utensil. Sighing, I gave up after mutilating half of her brain. I believe the last thing she saw before dying due to the severe head trauma, was a strand of her brain slide off of my fork into her lap. Her eyes twitched to the side then failed to close--ever again.

I went and got a spoon from my kitchen and

scooped at her brain as though it were some delicacy of a soup, and then I think I went a little haywire and started violently jamming my spoon into her brain…my memory is a bit shabby after that.

I must've been in my frenzy while I started stabbing her one of her breasts with the fork… I think I shoved the other breast into her stomach--that's what finally got me over the edge with a mind-blowing orgasm.

"Samantha Claire!" My mom practically shouted over the phone.

Suddenly squeezing the breast I now was holding close to mine, I could feel the frozen nipple almost break off. "Sorry Mom, I'm a horrid multi-tasker."

"I'll say. Why don't you call me back when you're done. I still would like to discuss me coming to visit you sometime. I still haven't seen your condo—and you've been there how long? Almost three years?"

"How about I call you tomorrow? I'm expecting a phone call from Edgar Stanley."

"Really? Why?"

"Oh just to be congratulated on a project I did or something." I lied.

"What project?"

"Mom, I've gotta go. I'll call you back soon."

"You said to--"

"Bye!"

Click. Jesus, the woman needed a life. I loved her and all, but I was busy, couldn't she fucking see that? I shook my head and looked back down at the frozen tit. Nothing damaged, good. I could start on my project tonight…

Then Saturday...oh God, I couldn't wait.

13

6:30 PM

I brushed my hair at first to the side, then
down the middle, then to the other side, and
still I couldn't fucking decide on the way I
wanted to look for that night. I felt giddy.
Excited. Angry at my fucking hair.

On my nightstand sat the decapitated head
of a girl I found at the back of my freezer. I
had been surprised I missed it when I cleaned
out the freezer. Then again, when I got into
my "moments" I tended to overlook a few things
(I quickly caught them later on, mind you.)

The head sat now thawing on a china white
dinner plate. Talk about having one's head
being served on a platter… I needed to have
an audience as I applied my make up--I was
too excited to be alone for the moment. The
eyes had been gouged out, leaving dark red
oozing holes, a few veins spilling out like
dead snakes. Brown blood had leaked down
slightly due to the thawing out of the flesh,
but in fact, the head was rather bone dry.
The hair looked brittle, almost like angel
hair pasta when its uncooked. The flesh had a

grey color with a slightly green and purple tinge, I assumed due to frost bite. The flesh looked puffy, bloated, and around her hallowed cheeks, slightly burnt.

Perched in its own decaying puddle of goo, a new liquid had begun to leave her mouth, making it almost look rabid. Her mouth fell open, all of her teeth ripped out. Dark red, almost black gums were uprooted, the roots of a few teeth could be seen sticking out like jagged little stones. Her tongue had shriveled up like a wet worm in the sun, and the roof of her mouth was peeling off. The jugular chord of her neck laid loosely beneath the head. When the head was de-thawing, I heard a sickening deflation sound as the jugular chord pushed out the rest of its frozen contents, vibrating the torn vocal chords slightly.

The song of the beckoning siren.

"You think I should part it this way?"

She didn't say anything, but I swear I could hear the liquid gurgle about the base of the slimy, puckered neck. The stench was wafting up now. I think maggots were already beginning to spawn in the right cavern of the cheek. It seemed a bit more full than the left--almost swollen, like an abscess of sorts. I stopped doing my hair, vaguely intrigued with the head.

"Have we been sneaking treats from the freezer?" I teased.

Never.

"Then where did my apple sorbet go?

You're accusing me of eating that healthy shit?

"You might've lived longer." I grinned then looked in the mirror. I pulled my hair back with a few silvery pins, lined with dark blue sapphires. This would work, a professional, yet causal bun. I let a few loose strands of black spill around my face. Perfect.

Cute.

"What? My comment? Or my hair? " I looked in the mirror again.

You're going to be late to your own invitation for dinner with...what's her name.

"Lisa. And you're just jealous. I will not be late, you fucking cunt. Shut your mouth." With that, I moved my hand over and placing a finger on the soggy, freezer burnt flesh of the chin, which now, for some reason seemed to start bloating, out, flesh peeling off like a bad sunburn, exposing black, rotted muscles and stringy white stuff that smelled a lot like fish beneath. I pushed that jaw up, closing the head's mouth. My attempt was in vain, it fell back open, but at least it was more closed than it started out as. A chunk of curdled flesh fell to the plate, leaving an oozing brown string of thick fluid still stuck to the face.

"Lovely," I said leaning down to look into her eyeless sockets. "You're gorgeous…" I whispered and then placed my lips over the rotted ones, or what was left. I pulled away, the lips now marred with my lipstick. I grabbed a tissue from the nearby box on my vanity set and dabbed at the brownish clear fluid now about my lips.

Was that a compliment to me?

"No, you fucking idiotic moron," I said in a sing song voice, then reapplied my lipstick. "That was to me. Now if you'll excuse me, this girl has a date to keep."

The hook is clean, you know…

I laughed as I stood up, looking quite chic and trendy. "I know," I glanced at the clock. "Gotta' run."

14

7:33 PM

I sat there, clad in a pair of black leather pants and a silvery silken blouse, my hair pulled up with the complimentary silvery pins. I looked ravishing, attaining looks from men of all types. I only had eyes for Lisa. My entire body *ached* for tonight. I had been waiting for so damn long! I was at the point (I'm sure you'll recognize this) where I felt like laughing, crying, and screaming all at once.

I idly fumbled with the napkin's ring holder. The restaurant was some "hip" new hot spot. I didn't even pay attention to the name, but I figured it'd impress Lisa. Why? Because I fucking could. Haven't we gone over this already? I do things because I can...and yet, why even that? Lately, that question had been on my mind. I can take lives, I can decide who will succumb to me or not, and yet...I can also stop.

This kept me awake at night. Most things did. Like… it's a sworn belief that teal and turquoise are two different shades of blue. FUCK THAT BULLSHIT! They are NOT! They are

the fucking same and the Goddamn painting com-
panies simply want to make profit off the low
life fuckwads that buy the bullshit coloring,
so they name it two different colors. MUCH
like wine and burgundy! It's bullshit and I
swear to God if I ever meet the designer, I'll
take his balls and rip them off, shove them
down his throat, so he can suck himself like
the dick he is.

   And if the designer is a chick? I'll...

   "Hi Ms....Sam," Lisa stammered. I glanced
up, my nails had left scratches in my napkin
ring.

   "You're late." I said evenly, my grey eyes
finally meeting hers. A vision of sheer perfection.

   It was then I knew I wanted her to dangle
on my hook as long as she could. I wanted to
paint my bathroom walls with her blood, let
her watch...I wanted her intestines to spill.
God, I wanted this girl.

   "Ohmygosh! I'm so sorry, I can explain."
She stammered, very caught off guard by my mo-
notonous statement.

   A smirk slid over my perfectly painted red
lips. "I was kidding, Lisa, we're supposed
to meet here at seven thirty, and it's seven
thirty-three. No biggie."

   The waiter that had brought Lisa over to my
table, clad in some very stylish looking vest
and black slacks combo, asked gregariously,
"Can I start you ladies off with something to
drink?"

   "I'll take a cosmopolitan," I said in a very
self assured tone. I wanted something light.
God knows that I didn't need to be drunk right
now. I was already feeling buzzed for dif-

ferent reasons other than alcohol entirely. Close. I was so damn close.

"I don't really know what to order. I mean, I guess I don't want to be a burden, you know?"

"Nonsense. Get whatever you'd like. Stop being so damn polite. You'll never make it in the business world if you think like that, darlin'."

She grinned, blushing. She cast her eyes over the restaurant, then over to the small drink menu sitting on our glass table. The table was held up with a miniature replica of Stonehenge, and around the table were little oil paintings of pans, (you know, the little half men half goat guys) fairies, and wood nymphs. I wanted to vomit.

Of all restaurants I picked the hippest, the flashiest, and the most popular one--I figured I'd impress the girl AND ruin my mental health at the same time. She looked absolutely stunning, clad in a black slinky dress that contrasted amazingly to her pale rosy skin just so. It also clung to that wicked body of hers.

"This place is amazing." My eyes flitted to her chest, slowly angling their way up that soft throat to those lips. But that nail polish on those finger nails! CHRIST! They would have to go.

And it was then that I realized, was I ever really being judged in the same manner I judged others? Sure people saw me, knew who I was, but did they know me? Does anyone know anybody? I looked at the girl across from me, some gorgeous woman who had no idea of the horrors I had in store for her, yet she sat, so innocent in front me, so unknowing. But *who* judges innocence? Society? By those fucking standards I'm Goddamn Mother Teresa. A saint, really.

Then I saw it.

That same fucking girl I saw all those months ago… the one who I kept for too long in the closet, the one who was desperate to eat some of her flesh just to survive. I saw the face of that rotting bitch I had ripped the intestines out of, I had chopped the head off and removed the eyes from. Lisa's face disappeared under the sudden sagging flesh, turning a grotesque grey and putrid green color. Her eyes slowly shrunk and shriveled down like white raisins, the juices from the inside gurgling out of her now deepening eye sockets. Her hair began to fall out, clump by clump, taking chunks of rotted scalp off with it, the skin peeling away like some horrific sunburn. The lips dried up and her tongue swelled up like some balloon, turning a dark purple color, boils forming on the sides created by (no doubt) the length of time she had been decomposing. Her cheeks hallowed out and slivers of grey and dull pink brain jelly seeped out those nearly empty eye sockets as the eyeballs themselves fell out, only dangling by rotting veins, that also looked like thick chords.

You still keep questioning, Sammy.

"Wouldn't you?" I shot back at the corpse before me. The tone of that…that voice bothered me.

You afraid of finding out that maybe this life isn't everything you thought it was? Everything in your life now Sammy, is so damn perfect and you know it. You're adored, you're getting away with some of the worst atrocities on mankind, and no one suspects a thing. Everything's just...

"Peachy-fucking-keen. Yeah, I know." Don't ask me why, and I won't even begin to explain it, but I didn't mind when the nickname, "Sammy" was used… it was almost… comforting?

So what's wrong, little girl? What's wrong now Sammy? Aren't you happy?

"Sam? Sam? Sam are you okay?"

I blinked, the corpse before me was gone, completely. Now sitting before was Lisa, still looking as stunning as ever. The eye juice that had leaked onto the table, leaving dark brown stains on the cloth was no more. It's as if it never was.

"Of course." My head felt light, my heart pounding in my chest. I calmed myself slowly by unfolding then re-folding the napkin over my legs. "Get a bit light headed if I don't eat a little something for a while."

Lisa smiled reassuringly and then nodded her head in that cute, girlish kind of way. Such a compassionate little intern. I wanted to rip her tongue out of her mouth and then fuck her up the cunt with it.

"Yeah, I know how that can be," Lisa said and then took a sip of her water. "My mom has hypoglycemia. She has to get a little something in her system every three to four hours, or so. But uh, what is heh, 'peachy-fucking-keen' if you don't mind my asking?"

"Oh. Uh, just an expression. Just excited to help out new talent and such."

"Aw, well, completely same here. Really, thank you for this."

"Not a problem."

"But, yeah... I would've never dreamed I'd be eating dinner with the famous Sam Ellis."

"Don't accentuate the L's," I said blandly, cutting in.

"Right. I mean, I just *loved* your work for the décor in that new place, Tinsel Town. You have this flare for vintage like..."

She seemed to drone on and on, hours perhaps. Though, in reality it was a matter of minutes. I nodded at all the appropriate times and smiled and laughed when it seemed fitting to do so. I was on auto-pilot. I even asked questions about her like, what school she went to (Insert some random preppy art school), what style she liked, (insert some cliché art medium here), inanities of that nature. Honestly, I found myself wondering about the skin from the breasts I had peeled off earlier this week while on the phone with my mother. They were ready by now, weren't they? I could use them (after tattooing the flesh a bit) as coasters for drinks. There was an idea.

And even then, the décor of my own place was failing to excite me. Once I was finished, what then? What then, indeed. There was always the Vogue Fashion Awards on VH1. None of those nitwits knew how to dress well, except maybe Gwenyth. But honestly, what was she *thinking* by playing Sylvia Plath in that movie? Sylvia was a dark character and Gwenyth? Well, she's just like some modern day Grace Kelly if you ask me. Speaking of which, we'd have to leave soon. *E!'s Best and Worst Dressed at the Oscars* was on tonight.

Just then Lisa laughed at the story she was telling me. Apparently, it was supposed to be what stupid people call, "a funny story."

I stared back in silence, my eyes as blank as the eyes that stared openly, immortalized in my shower.

She watched me a moment and then cleared her throat, obviously feeling uncomfortable. She got up to excuse herself to go to the bathroom. I laughed politely, but it was too damn late. I had missed my cue to act *normal*--as usual. And as she remained in the restroom? I pulled open my purse and within the blink of an eye worked my magic over her drink. Enough of this bullshit—time to get things moving.

"So your fiancé sounds like a real nice guy," I said tentatively as she sat back down, having returned from her little 'powder room' break. She nodded, but I could see I was losing her.

"He's my boyfriend actually... We've only discussed marriage. Nothing there yet." She then took a healthy drink which only served to secretly please me.

"Right." I then inwardly cursed at myself--I had made that statement about three times now. I was seriously blowing it.

Think! Think! What's your fucking problem?! I thought bitterly at myself, thankful the food (I couldn't remember ordering) arrived.

The mythological place was growing to be a complete bore to me. I thought I saw Puck, or Pan, or one of those Greek shitheads waltz by with some wooden flute sticking out of his mouth. I poked at my salad. It was healthy, it was green, it was crunchy and exactly the way I wanted it. So was the side of apple slices. Everything was perfect.

"So Sam, you've been kind of...quiet." Lisa

finally said, wrapping some linguini about her fork. I stared at that hideous color on those nails again.

"I'm sorry. Work's been so busy lately, y'know? Seems like every main entertainment company in the world wants me to review their décor."

"I can understand," Lisa said gently, still not completely buying my façade. At least, I didn't think she was. I was starting to doubt my perceptions on people anymore.

"Well, anyway, that's neither here nor there, right darlin'? How about taking a look at some of my sketches and such now?" I put on the ol' Sam Ellis grin and then took a bite of my salad.

"Y'know… I'm not feelin' so hot. Can we look over some of those foot notesh' an' sketches… shome' other time?" Lisa's words were really starting to slur. Show time.

"Sure thing. Lemme get the tab and we'll head out." True to my word, I paid the ridiculous bill (since when is goddamned pasta worth thirty-seven bucks?) and we exited the restaurant. "You know, you really don't look so hot—did you drive?"

"No. Tooka' cab." She really was getting hit hard by those Quaaludes. I loved those things.

"Here, I'll give you a ride. It's the least I can do if you're not feeling so hot." And before she could register what was going on? I helped her into the passenger seat of my car. Within a few moments, we were out of the parking lot and onto the main street.

"Really I think it mighta' been shomethin' I ate." Lisa mumbled out.

"I doubt that. I'm doing perfectly fine."

"You ordered different…"

"But, that was a five star restaurant." I flashed her the devil's grin now. "Actually, the reason why you're feeling so shitty is because I slipped a Quaalude into your drink, while you were in the bathroom, Lisa. So don't blame the fucking restaurant--I paid a shit load on the drinks alone, tonight."

"Wha?"

"You fucking heard me, you cunt fuck. I know that Quaaludes, while they make you sluggish and alter your perception, do not really affect your hearing."

"I… Sham'… I wanna go home."

"To your fiancé?" Boyfriend, whatever—like I gave a shit. "Well, that's not on the schedule. However, what is would consist of me fucking you up your tight little cunt so hard with my homemade dildo until I rip your insides apart. Don't worry though, you'll be alive to feel your flesh tear, your ovaries pop, and I might even rupture an intestine or two."

"Sham..." She suddenly screamed out. I slowed down, then came to a stop at a red light. A random cop car was patrolling by. Wow, the city really was on a crack down. "That's not funny! I want out! NOW!"

"I'm sorry darlin', that just isn't gonna happen. Now shut up kindly."

Suddenly, to my serious dismay, the bitch started screaming. It made me wince, but I was prepared. I quickly reached into my purse and pulled out my nail file. I jabbed it once, rather hard into her throat, ruining her larynx. She could no longer speak, or scream for that matter.

The blade of the nail file broke off. "Piece of shit," I muttered. Her scream was cut short with a gurgling, then hoarse sound. I could hear the raspy shaking of her vocal chords as blood and air blocked her voiceless sound. She lazily, clumsily clawed at her throat, only pushing the blade in further.

"Don't do that," I said darkly. "You'll cut into your jugular and then you're REALLY fucked."

She stopped. The drugs in her system mixed with the alcohol made her slow, sluggish, unable to really comprehend all that was occurring. She merely sat there limply—either in some state of shock, some state of being drug induced, or perhaps she realized her own fate. After all, when I mean business I fucking mean business.

The cop car simply drove on its merry way, away from us. I then drove on as the light turned green.

"Ah, perfect." I then said and moved one hand over to Lisa, squeezing a robust breast rather violently. She groaned, at least tried to. It came out like air deflating from a tire. I squeezed even harder, my fingers pushing in so tightly that I could feel the pop of blood vessels. She writhed like some retarded, blind worm beneath me, utterly silent, only that hoarse breathing and scraping.

I then hung a left, reaching my apartment complex. She was crying now, tears streaming down her face, make up smeared. God, she looked so fucking hot right now. I had to admit, I was starting to get wet. Whatever I was feeling in the restaurant definitely had passed. Maybe I was just getting ready for my period.

I parked my car in its space and walked cheerfully, over to Lisa's side. I opened the door and unbuckled her, took her out and helped her up. She moved like some hefty drunken ballet dancer. I slung her against me and I could hear her soft whimpers. I gingerly ran my hand down her full stomach, feeling the soft fleshy fat yield to my touch. I walked, slightly strained (as gorgeous as she was, she was a little bit heavier than I had counted on) and began to walk up the steps to my place.

My muscles were tensed against her weight, and I felt myself break out into a sweat. I was vaguely out of breath and deep down I realized this is why most serial killers are men.

Fuck that. Maybe I'm a man trapped in a woman's body, huh?

I smirked at that random thought and finally reached my apartment door.

Suddenly, the door across from mine opened and I froze. It was my neighbor, Mr. Lundun, or Landow, or Lanky, or whatever. Cutting through Lisa's soft feminine scent of perfume came the nasty scent of dog, dog shit, and cigarettes. Gotta love humanity, right? Fucking disgusting.

"Hello Miss Ellis," he said with a small white puff ball of a dog in his hands. He was maybe in his fifties. His face had so many wrinkles he looked like a giant, walking crack in an earthquake ridden sidewalk. I thought if the wind might blow too hard, he might just turn to dust and blow away with it. The decrepit man grinned at me, making his face

crack even more. "See you gotta' a friend
with ya' tonight, huh?"

"Uh yeah. She had a bit too much to drink.
I'm just letting her stay over until she so-
bers up some."

"Alright then. You have a nice evening."
His little white cotton ball of a dog began
to yip. I felt a twitch start above my right
eye.

My neighbor what's-his-face was already
starting down the stairs, unable to notice
Lisa's attempt to hold onto the door frame.

I pulled her in and closed my door quietly.
I then brought her back towards my bedroom,
catching the blinking light on my answering
machine. I'd check that later.

I draped her on my bed and then crawled over
her, running my fingers down her voluptuous
form. She was shaking with fear, tears falling down her cheeks uncontrollably.

"Oh Lisa," I sighed. "We're gonna have some
fun! Now enjoy it, you cunt sucking whore."

I moved behind her, kicking off my own pumps
and sat her up, propping some pillows up behind
her. She caught sight of the severed head I
had left on my vanity set and tried once again
to scream. I couldn't help but laugh. Lisa's
face looked almost just like the dead head's,
with the exception of Lisa being alive and the
head being, well, dead.

I then headed over to my dresser drawer and
opened it up. My apartment was totally silent-
-I was missing *E!'s Best and Worst Dressed at
the Oscars*! I grabbed my remote and flipped my
TV on. Sean Penn had just finished showing off
his Armani suit. Brad and Angelina were next,
their arms linked romantically. She looked

great in her Gucci dress, he looked like shit in his Vivienne Westwood suit. Lisa, still very much on my bed, was trying to struggle, but she made no progress whatsoever. She was too sluggish, too disoriented, yet, amazingly enough still very conscious. Then again, she was a big girl.

I then reached my hand inside my drawer and pulled out a pair of pliers. I moved over on the bed next to Lisa and lifted one of her hands up. "Now darlin', as much as I think you're fuckin' hot, and as much as you get my own little cunt wetter than anything, your finger nail polish has been annoying the fuck out of me." I said in a sing-song voice, most likely mimicking Susan Wells from work.

Lisa was shaking and begging as I lifted up one hand in front of her. I placed the pliers on her soft flesh and then squeezed down. First I cut through the first layer of skin, then deeper, hitting the second and third layers of flesh. Blood started to ooze out, and then I cut through the fat, making more blood and a slightly yellow/clear color stream out as well. I went harder, concentrating, cutting at the joint of the first finger. Her other fingers were wiggling like worms then closing tightly in pain. The first finger, the one I was working on, was shaking even worse than the rest, wriggling and shaking violently as nerve endings shot off one by one.

Deeper, through the fat, then the muscle tissue and then finally to the bone where a sickening SNAP was heard and there, the bare finger fell off. A bloody nub was left. Where her first finger once was, blood was gushing down now. I'd have to burn these sheets later.   Normally I'd use my cherished bathtub, but the *Best and Worst Dressed* was on!

I'm sure if she could've screamed by now, she would've, but she was simply writhing in pain, more tears--she looked faint, pale. She looked like she might be sick.   Her mouth opened and closed like some fish out of water.

"Darlin', that hue of red is just an atrocity to even wear.   And worse yet, you've got it on your fingers?!"

Suddenly, Joan Rivers' voice came on, scratchy as fuck and all.   "Oh, oh my GAWD! Just look at Halle Berry! Ugh! Just up-most perfection! Oh God, she's such a doll! Ugh!" I glanced back, checking out to see what Miss Berry was wearing, pausing in the castration of Lisa's fingers.

I frowned. I didn't think the gown was all too exquisite.   Honestly, I expected Gucci to do much better,like that one dress they did for Selma Hayek.

I turned back around and suddenly received a very sharp pain on my shoulder. I couldn't help but scream out.   THE BITCH HAD FUCKING BIT ME!!!

I pulled her off and in doing so, a chunk of my flesh was taken along with her.   "Oh you MOTHER fucking CUNT WHORE!   You're gonna' be SO MOTHER fucking sorry! Do you KNOW how much I paid for this dress?! Do YOU?!" Blood was now pouring down my right arm, my flesh was throbbing. How fucking deep was it?

She spit the chunk of flesh out onto my bed. It looked like some piece of very pale raw meat with muscle tissue and fat cells.   I thought I even saw a vein in there. Fuck.

"You're gonna' be so fucking sorry." I then

struck her hard across the face, not caring about my pain momentarily.

I then took her hand as she fell back, breathing hard and begin to finish cutting off each and every finger. I twisted the pliers about her thumb, screwing the skin off first, digging down to the bone, and then corkscrewed around and around, popping her thumb off obscenely. A jagged large white bone from her thumb stuck out, wriggling. Shavings of bloody flesh hung loosely from the desecrated bone.

"HA!" I laughed out. I then grabbed that hand of hers, now completely void of fingers. Blood was everywhere, some of it creating goopy black and dark red chunks. Her hand was swollen now, the thumb bone jaggedly sticking through. Ripped strands of flesh dangled loosely, a few veins could be seen, raw and exposed.

I took her stubby hand down and brought it to her cunt through her dress. I then began to fuck her with it. I rammed her nub of a newly deformed hand against her clothed pussy as hard as I could, making her jerk violently. The fingers rolled off the bed with my maniacal movements.

"Fuck you," I breathed out, fucking her. More hoarse gurgles emitted from her. I then moved her hand back from herself so harshly and roughly that it made a sickening crack. I glanced up to her shoulder, part of her bone was now sticking through the skin, as if it came out just to say hello to me.

Her arm hung at some weird, limp angle. The skin then ripped, fat and blood was pushed out like when you pop a zit and the white puss from the inside flies out and hits the glass of the mirror.

I sucked in a deep breath and then grabbed her other hand, I began to hack off each finger. This time, not exactly using the pliers the way they were meant. I simply kept on beating the first finger so harshly that finally I crushed the bone, then I broke the skin and hit it harder and harder. Striking. Finally, stringy bits of flesh and muscle were all that held that finger on and then I clipped it.

I glanced up to see Lisa's face and it was contorted into such pain that finally, she had passed out. Good.

I finished cutting off her fingers anyway and then picked them all up. The ruined ones I'd burn. The ones I had managed to cut off nicely would work as candles, cover them in some formaldehyde then dip them in wax and viola! A perfect fixture for any home.

"Ugh! Oh God LOOK! It's Johnny Depp! He appears to be in a lovely Versace suit, but the hair, darling! It has GOT to go! Not the look for you, boy. Ugh! Swear ta' GAWD it's called a hair dresser Johnny, yeesh!" Joan Rivers went on in the background.

I took this time to clean up my room and take care of my own wound. I cleaned it and bandaged it and then placed the fingers (I had managed to keep seven of them) in some saran wrap and put them in the freezer for later. I then took out some lean chicken breasts to de-thaw--I'd have them for dinner tomorrow night, and took out a Snapple. I popped it open and checked my messages.

"Sam, this is your mothe--"
Skip.
"Ms. Samantha Ellis, you are the winner of

Life Time Sweepsta--"

Skip.

"Hey! This is Jenny. I saw you at the club the other night, and I talked with you some. You gave me your number and I'm just now getting a chance to call you…so maybe we ought to…go out for drinks, or something? Anyway, I'll give you my number. 385-7233. Alright, bye."

I listened to the message carefully. Jenny… Jenny… who the fuck was that? I remembered going out to the clubs the other night. I must've thought she was cute or I wouldn't have given her my number. I'll check into her later.

"Sam, this is Edgar Stanley. I received the report and it's good to go. I'm calling you because a new dance club is being built over on Pine and Third Street. They are a multi-billion dollar corporation coming in from Europe, trying their hand here in the States. They want you to maybe give them some sketches. They've heard about you and if they like you, they want you to do their interiors. Samantha, we need this deal, it would really put us on the map internationally. Think about it."

I finished my Snapple and tossed it. I washed my hands and then headed back into my bedroom, luckily, just in time to see Gwenyth Paltrow walk over the red carpet, looking glamorous in a Chanel pearl white silken, hip hugging gown. I glanced down at Lisa, hearing her slowly began to stutter. Indeed, the fun was just about to begin…

I headed over to my closet and got undressed. I placed my clothes into the hamper, in which I would have to throw my dress out.

It was utterly ruined. The bitch. I then searched my hoards of shoe boxes and found what I was looking for. I pulled out a black shiny leather belt that almost seemed to carry a harness on it. I had stitched the creation together myself.

It was actually a strap on. But not just any kind of strap, oh, no-no. Haven't we already discussed my perfect creativity? Or were you too busy still questioning my life style? The strap on wasn't made with a dildo. It was made with one of the ribs I had taken out of a girl a while back. I had polished it, sharpened the tip to a point and coated it with some enamel. It was sturdy, gleaming white, and sharp as a fucker. I had always wanted to use it, but for some reason or another, I got caught up with doing other things.

What can I say? Us artists can be flakey.

I headed over to Lisa who was still groggy and then emitted a low gurgled groan of pain. I think by now, the bitch had to know she was dying. She cupped her hands to her breasts and I stepped into my homemade strap on. I fastened and tightened it. The rib was long, perhaps near about nine inches? I had shortened it some, just for shits and giggles.

I then headed over to her and pulled her flat onto the bed. I peeled off her dress, and then got to her panties and bra, exposing her nude form. Her curves were so prominent…so full. Her nipples weren't erect, but given time they would be.

I grinned the devil's own grin over her. The TV behind me lighting up the dark room dully, casting a silvery glow on my tense, tight, in shape slender body. I stood over her, my own breasts pert, my nipples hard and what was even harder was my stiff "cock."

I slid over her and pushed her thick thighs apart, feeling her tremble beneath me. I began to slide the rib into her, breathing in deeply as I did so, watching her face. Her eyes went from red, glassy and puffy, to wide and pained, scared as a little rabbit. The little white rabbit.

I then slammed into her, making her emit a hoarse shriek of pain. Already a warm fluid began to flow over her thighs and onto my pubic hair and cunt. I ripped into her, feeling the sharpened rib pierce through her vaginal wall, tearing the flesh from her inside, and stabbing right into her ovaries. I pumped again and again, creating a rhythm.

The rib slid in deeper each time, blood now gushed out freely, so wet and hot and sticky. I was covered in sweat now, ramming into her. I then leaned over and pressed my lips fiercely over hers, kissing her heatedly. My pelvis still gyrated into her insanely, with abandon. The rib then ripped up her uterus lining and hit something kind of hard. It made a slight "tick" type of sound, muffled by being buried into her body.

I groaned. I think I had hit her spine or perhaps her pelvic bone. I ground into her harder, now hearing more sloshing than I should. By now, she was on the verge of losing consciousness, literally getting her insides ripped right out. And yet… I fucked her, hard, fast, deep. In. Out. In. Out. Harder. Faster. My breathing labored, my heart pounding.

Deeper! Her breasts shaking in front of me.

I leaned down, kissing her again, this time I bit her lower lip and pulled back, ripping off the mid section of her bottom lip, making her mouth bleed profusely. I could see her teeth now, even though her lips were closed, through the hole I placed into her. I fucked her harder, harder…more sloshing. Soon it was so easy to ram into her not because she was loose. Not by any means. I just had ripped open such a hole within her now I was sure I could fit both of my hands up inside her.

I then stopped. I wasn't getting off whatsoever. Not even slightly. I mean, yeah, I was enjoying myself like some hedonist, but this was meaning nothing to me. Slowly I pulled out. Bits of flesh and something that looked like stringy thick blood strands were stuck to the rib. Something fleshy, pulpy and almost green colored was stuck to the tip, pierced through. It smelled putrid. I pulled off the strap on and then got down to her cunt. I could see masses of flesh piled up.

Something was sticking out of her cunt. I decided to pull on it--why not, right? So I did, and I kept tugging and tugging and tugging. I heard a gurgled strangling sound come from Lisa as I literally pulled her insides out of her. She had just enough time for me to pull out her lower intestine through her cunt before she finally died--eyes wide open. They rolled back into her head, leaving only the whites visible. Her mouth open, blood still seeping out.

I looked at the intestine, it was long and slimy and grey. It looked a bit mutilated, probably from my fucking. It was kind of like a hose with bumps and strands of bloody veins.

Spidery like veins crawled all across it, and the smell was horrid. I looked closer and squeezed on it, suddenly shit began to drip out, first wet and runny, filled with blood, then harder, not completely digested yet. I headed to my bathroom and put the lower, shit filled intestine into the bathtub, more putrid shit came out as if on an involuntary reaction, it was kind of dark green with bits of noodles in it from tonight's dinner. I then headed back to my room and lifted Lisa off of my bed with more of a struggle than before.

Now she was just dead weight. I headed slowly over to my prized bathtub and caught my breath as with one hand I opened the shower curtains wider, exposing my giant hanging fish hook. I slung her forward, this time, the hook caught on her belly, ripping it open. A fart sound came out, along with squishy plops. The rest of her intestines fell out, along with a punctured kidney. She hung, by her belly, her breasts and face looking down towards the tub. Her tongue stuck out and a bit of fat now dripped off of her exposed liver and stomach and fell into the tub. Snot and mucus fell from her nose and mouth.

Her arms hung limply as did her legs as she simply dangled on my hook, like so many before her. Her guts simply swung gently back and forth, like some red and grey hypnotic pendulum. I picked up her stomach, gripping a few of the large reddish-black veins that fed into the pink, wet, fatty covered pouch of a muscle, and squeezed it. The rest of her undigested food squirted out, it was some weird yellow and dark brown color. Blood dripped everywhere, and suddenly I think the rest of her nerves went off because the larger intestine pushed out the rest of the digested food, looking once again like very wet shit, with food chunks in it. I could even make out a peanut, part of a hamburger bun, and…I looked closer, a chewed up black olive.

I stared at her. This was it? This is what I had been waiting for all week? I felt…empty. I felt hollow.

All of this had meant nothing.

15

7:02 AM

I had wanted to call in sick to work the
next day, but couldn't. After all, I had the
intern's body still hanging in my 1930's bathtub. I got ready, as usual, feeling as if I
were to get dressed with my eyes closed, I
would still know where each and every thing
is. I would still look just as natural as always.

I got into my car, feeling still so vacant
and hollow, and drove to work. I seemed to
float up to my desk, and numbly answered questions. I participated in the office gossip.
Even when Susan Wells came by, I felt *nothing*.
Not even disgust, or my favorite...loathing.

When Mr. Boring spoke to me, I answered back
like some automaton. I couldn't figure out
what was wrong. I couldn't...I just couldn't.

I sat at my desk, reading over layouts for
designs. Then I reread them and reread them.
Nothing made any sense in front of my eyes.
Was I drugged? Drunk? Tired? No. I just
felt like I wasn't anything at all.

Only when the designs in front of me seemed

to change and I saw *her* face again—that's when I felt something! That BITCH! I stared at it, now feeling obviously something, complete and utter disbelief. Confusion? It was… what I am going to now simply refer to as, the voice. But whose?

See Sammy? You feel vacant.

"Good observation, Sherlock."

Have you ever wondered why you watch so many other people's lives, Sammy? Haven't you ever come to the conclusion that maybe you watch the surreal world of Hollywood because you can relate to it so well? You're an actress too, Sammy. You're fake.

"Yeah? So is every other mother fucking human out there. At least I still act on what I feel."

Do you?

"What's that supposed to mean?"

I don't know. It seems to me you choose to place yourself above the human race.

"That's insane. Are you implying that you think I'm better than human?"

No Sammy…you're implying that.

"That's so fucking off the wall."

Am I Sammy? What other person out there do you know that can do the things you do and not feel one thing? Not an ounce of remorse? An ounce of regret? Face it, Sammy. You can't even feel pleasure anymore. What do you feel? Anything?

I was silent now, staring at that head. Staring at the voice. The flesh was a dark green and yellowish color. Maggots writhed and wriggled out from the gaping, holes on both cheek sides. The eyeballs were completely shriveled away now, and the tongue flapped like loose paper. The rotted flesh was cracked, caked with dry blood, it was amazing that the lips even moved. A few strands of hair remained left on the head, exposing a scab-covered scalp. Patches and chunks of the scalp had decayed away, exposing a putrid, maggot-ridden grey and somewhat pinkish white brain. A brown liquid slopped about inside the brain, dripping slowly out from the ears and eyes. The nose was completely gone, showing off tan and pink cartilage. Dried boogers stuck about the upper lip, causing the skin to flake off.

"Wait a fucking second. What about all the *others* who have done the exact same thing, huh? Like Jeffery Dahmer, Ted Bundy, John Wayne Gacy, Albert Fish, Aileen W--"

Are you them, Sammy? No. You're Samantha Ellis. You can't account for someone you've never even met. In fact, the only person you can ever answer for is yourself. This brings you full circle, back to living in the whole surreal Hollywood world, Sammy. A world of false dreams and realities. Your escape from life. Now tell me, Sammy, are you happy? Is your life…art? Like you always wanted?

"No." I whispered, hating the girl's head for being so damned right. Hating the voice.

What's the point, Sammy, in doing what you do when there's no one to share it with?

"Fuck you. Who the hell are you to judge me, huh? No one! I fucking KILLED you! You have no right to say any of this to me! NO FUCKING RIGHT! I'm living just perfectly well, okay? I have a great job, good relationship with my mother, I'm rich, I get to do anything I want--indulge in anything I want. I GET anything

I want! I have it ALL!"

"Sam?"

I turned to hide the decayed head that was talking on my desk! I glanced up —at the fake as fucking press on nails bitch, Susan.

"Yeah." My right eye flinched slightly at the use of my name as if my physical self took on that loathing I carried when my mental self was too lethargic.

"You okay? Missed ya' in the coffee room this morning."

"Yeah. Just…long night."

"Oh yeah! I hear ya' there, girly. Once I was at this club and..."

"Susan?"

"Yes?"

"Please. I need to write some reports." I didn't even care about her suspicious look. I was tired, drained, and something felt horribly wrong. But what? The head was gone. The rest of the day droned on, and I felt like I was floating in some surreal dream, like one of *The Stepford Wives*, nod here, smile there, answer this, decline that. I was stuck in a fucking bad joke.

When people commented on Lisa's not showing up that day, I didn't pay attention. I spent most of the time either secluded to my desk, or in the women's bathroom, vomiting.

After my third vomit, in which only the clear bile and some pink stringy things came up, I headed back to my desk. Susan passed by, giving me some little catty look, but being as indifferent as I was. I simply slid into my cubicle and stared at the clock. I watched as it tick, tick, ticked its slow damn way just a LITTLE bit closer to when I get off. I stared at my blank computer screen. All day I had been there, and all day my computer screen hadn't been used at all. It was as blank as how my mind felt--the perfect match to my God-damn monitor. Blank, blank, BLANK!

Finally I made some excuse about seeing a client and I was up and out of there. I didn't even say bye to anyone as I bolted towards the elevators. The fuckers could rot in hell for all I cared. I needed to be back home... I needed to be away from everyone. I needed to think.

16

9:31 PM

I laid quietly on my bed, the gentle sound of a flickering candle off to my right, the sounds of traffic surrounding my apartment. No TV on. Nothing of the movie/fashion industry was showing tonight, so why even bother? I hate music. And I had unplugged my phone and turned my cell phone off. I simply laid on my bed, completely naked, staring at my ceiling. When I had gotten home I had managed to bleach the hell out of my sheets and then folded them up as small as possible and placed them in the back of the closet. I'd burn them later, when the trash burning restriction lifted.

Lisa's body still hung, now dried and decaying, in my bathtub. Her weight was starting to tug on her skin, stretching it out some, making her look like some human, feminine form of gored silly putty. The scent in my bathroom was beyond rancid so I kept the door closed and a towel stuffed beneath it. I cleaned the hell out of my apartment afterwards and used my guest bathroom to shower.

All of this done before 9 pm. And now, here

I am… silent, laying in silence letting my thoughts run. And that, they did.

I remembered once when I was a little girl and my mother took me to the woods to enjoy nature for a weekend. I used to watch all the trees as we drove by them in the darkness, wondering if Dracula would actually come out to take me away. If he would show me his secrets to immortality. I wondered how many other people those trees, themselves, had seen, met, and actually remembered. How many trees had witnessed the most horrible of car accidents, housed criminals…how many of those trees purposely tricked people, made them get lost in the woods, and then starved them to death and hid the bodies as if it never happened?

I used to watch the night sky when I was a little girl, wishing that a UFO would take me away, and I'd never return. Or perhaps, maybe the ground would open up and just swallow me, placing me into black nothingness. I used to wonder if while someone wished on a shooting star, did that falling star come to earth? If so, did it ever land on someone, killing them instantly? I always wanted to see that happen.

All my life I've always wanted to see something terrible happen to someone else, like being brutally killed in a violent car wreck.

I guess I got tired of waiting in rush hour traffic.

Sex had never been all it was cracked up to be. Never once did I scream out someone's name so loud that a neighbor had to come and knock on my door. I always made them scream, whether they liked it or not. The thought of sex… with something warm, something… alive, something able to reciprocate just doesn't seem to be able to sit well within me. When you boil it all down, I guess I like control--what person doesn't? And if I can't control their every whim, I have no interest with them what-so-ever. Life means nothing without control.

When I was young, I thought maybe I had a super power just waiting to emerge one day. Maybe I could fly, or maybe I would breath fire, maybe I could lift things with my mind…maybe I could just finally let go of everything and…

And what?

I was silent, the thought beginning to push its way out of my mind, but I restricted it. I didn't want it there. For some reason it made me feel

(human)

strange to think about.

I gently trailed my fingers over my taut stomach. It felt even slimmer, most likely due to the vomiting spells I had for whatever reason today. I worked out, I ate right, I had a great job, I had friends, I had a good relationship with my mother--WHAT'S PICKING AT MY BRAIN?!

Unhappiness.

"Who the fuck said that?" I sat up suddenly, glancing about my candle-lit room.

Though I had an inkling as to who it was… what it was. The voice.

Look in the mirror.

I glanced over to my vanity set, and in the reflection, instead of seeing my perfectly clear, smooth, and beautiful complexion I saw *her* again, the head, just as decayed as ever, if not worse. But whose? I didn't recognize her. She was like all the rest.

"What the fuck makes you the expert on such things?"

C'mon Sammy, stop denying it. You're as thick as a brick. How much longer are you go-ing to go on pretending to overlook the fact that you too feel fear? That you too, have needs? That you too are--

"No one asked for your opinion, maggot face."

Oh yeah, Sammy? Then why am I here?

"That's what I've been trying to figure out! I DON'T KNOW! But ever since I've seen you, things have been real shitty y'know? So go and decay in someone else's mirrors, computer screens, whatever. I want my life back."

What life is that Sammy? The killer? The interior design consultant/slash closet les-bian? The "adoring" daughter? The liar? The "actress"? The perfectionist? Which one?

"Shut the fuck up."

Uh oh, did I hit too close to home, huh, Sammy? Guess what, "darlin'", guess fucking what?

I stared at the corpse in the mirror. That self-satisfied rotting face. I wanted the voice to burn, watch all the flesh melt and twist off, watch the hair sizzle and the bones begin to flake away.

C'mon, guess!

"You're being juvenile."

You're being deluded.

"Fine. What?"

Who else calls you Sammy?

"I'm the only one who can call me that, bitch." *Exactly. So who do you think I am? Get it?*

"Get the fuck outta here."

Deep down you know who I am, some small part. Not your fucking conscious--you found a way to murder that bitch a long time ago, I'm not "the voice" you tend to refer to me as, and I'm not your "sixth sense" or "intuition" I'm you.

I stared at the mirror, closely to see if my eye was twitching or not. Suddenly, I didn't even care what Gwenyth Paltrow was going to wear of the premiere at the Red Carpet show on *E!* that night and that scared me. How could I just not care at all?. Without warning, I thrust my naked body up off the bed, and let out a scream of sheer anger (at least… I could've sworn that it was anger…) and pounded my fists against the glass of my mirror.

It shattered into hundreds of little pieces, my hands were now bloody and raw, staining the glass with my own crimson flow. I kept beating at it, beating at it, beating at it. That damn corpse was still there! That fucking voice! I kept screaming, until I could make no more sound, no glass to destroy left, and no more flesh to rip off my hands. I fell to my knees, ribbons of silver, red stained glass sliced up my legs...I just…didn't…care.

And with my voice hoarse, blood now covering my shivering naked form, I tried like hell to cry. I was in an incredible amount of pain, but only physically. Only physically. No tears would run down my cheeks. Only sweat. I wiped it away with a bloody hand, shoving a shard of glass deeper into my palm. I flinched and then laid on my back, in the glass, feeling like my whole form was being injected into by a thousand tiny needles. I felt like I was on fire.

I looked up to my ceiling, picking at the shard of glass that had wedged so deeply into my palm, blood dripping out and all over my face, my breasts, my throat… and I felt that fire of pain beneath me.

"I am the phoenix." I said quietly, I said to no one, except to the dead corpse that still hung in my bathroom. Lara, Lucy, Lisa, or whatever. "I am the phoenix."

And I laid there, for what seemed like hours and for all I know, it could've possibly been, waiting. Just waiting to catch ablaze, waiting to turn to ash. Waiting to rise again.

"I am the phoenix."

Here I was at a stand still. In front of me stood the whitest, most pure horse I had ever seen. And behind me was the opening to a cave. I glanced to the horse and then stepped towards it. The horse knelt as best a horse could and allowed me to climb atop its massive back. The horse then trampled and glided towards that open cave.

The rocks glistening like diamonds. And people were cheering. I was to ride off into the sunset. Further and further into the blackness of the cave. The cave was getting warmer and my horse suddenly began to shake. I kicked at its side, trying to make it move faster through the now, pitch black, hot and humid cave.

My horse then fell, breaking its leg on a rock. I clung tight and then climbed off. I had to leave the animal there. I needed to go deeper into the cave.

I heard my mother call for me, and spun

around to catch sight of my mother, impaled by one of the stalagmites of the cave, the horse now gone. I came back, hearing my mother beg, plead for forgiveness…

I stood above her, silent, watching the tears flow from her cheeks. She held up pictures of me when I was a little girl, she begged to be forgiven. It would have been so easy for me to lift her off that sharp stalagmite. Stranegly, she was smiling at me. I just stared back at her. The pictures she showed me suddenly turned into pictures of bloody corpses that I had taken during my "sessions" with the girls.

I had never seen such fear in my mother's eyes as I did then. I needed to lift her up, to get her off that horrible rock that was almost poking straight through her back. And yet, it would be even easier to…

I shoved her back onto that stalagmite, making blood bubble up and out of her mouth. I killed her and I laughed as blood gushed from her like some volcano. Sick gurgling noises, like some drowning cat, bubbled up from her chest. Her throat then swelled up like a hot air balloon, filling with blood. I watched in utter amazement, and it was like I was outside of myself. I saw me, a sadistic grin on my face as my mother's throat got bigger and bigger. I could first see stretch marks forming on the pale skin, like little pearl colored lines, then they grew darker and darker, turning from a pallid white-pink to a deep magenta, then dark red, then violent purple.

SPLAT!

Her throat exploded, and gallons and gallons of blood flew every which way. Bits of her muscle tissue hit the side of my face. All I could do was watch as blood pumped out of her profusely. The floor was sloshed with blood, the cave filling up fast. I ran further back into that hot, humid cave, and luckily, I found some perfect porcelain white rocks to climb on top of to get away from the pooling blood.

I glanced up and had just enough time to scream as suddenly, the cave collapsed on me, smashing me like some insect. Blood, guts, ooze, and whatever else squirted out of me, like a crushed tomato.

And there, I saw that the cave I had been in was no cave, but some giant, hideous, de-caying, rotting head. It was that "girl"... the voice talking at me in the mirror haunting me in my life. At work. At home. Everywhere it seemed. But no, it wasn't...

The skin began to grow up, hallowed, grey cheeks filling in. Shriveled, sunken eyes fill-ing back up with puss. Scraggily hair became full, midnight black and luxurious. Soon, the head was complete--it was me.

"General Hoff fired it off, Sam."

"Lt. Banner carried the rammer," I respond-ed to myself.

"Hold onto nothing as fast as you can."

"It's gonna go quick."

"Everything's temporary."

"Even me?"

"Even you."

17

6:53 AM

I was fucking late to work. So fucking late it was ridiculous. Hopefully Mr. Stanley would take notice that I had been working so extra hard on this new file he asked me to do. Still, the dream I had had the night before, it had to be one of the most bizarre ones I'd ever had. I was not feeling myself.

My hand ached horrifically from the incident with the mirror, things were blurring together. I wasn't really sure what day it was, or even the month, actually. I just forgot to look. I was busy, okay? The corpse of what's-her-face still hung in my bathroom. My whole apartment now smelled like death and fecal matter. I hadn't bothered to clean up the glass from my mirror. My blood on it attracted all sorts of insects (though they most likely came from that bitch's body in my bathroom). I stepped on a fat cockroach with my bare foot.

I killed it with a satisfying crunch, feeling its wiggly antennae wave about as its last nerves went off. It was wet, squishy, and yet hard and crunchy all at once. I was reminded of an apple. I headed to my fridge, merely

143

wiping the roach guts off on my perfectly ivory white carpet.

I opened the fridge and the smell of rotting fruit greeted me. I held my nose and tried not to gag. Guess I had left my bag of apples too long in there.

How long was too long? I was SO fucking late. I quickly pulled on whatever outfit I could find--it was classy enough, but smelled like mold and decay. It had probably picked up the scent of the apartment and embedded it within its threads. I sprayed myself down with some perfume (I can't remember the last time I showered... I'm trying to bring the "grunge" look back into play. If Cameron Diaz could get away with it in the movie, *Being John Malkovich*, then so could I.)

I left my place, my mind askew. I almost forgot where my assigned parking space was, and accidentally ran two red lights, swearing to GOD they were green. No cops were about, so I felt like Lady Luck was shining down on me today.

I FINALLY made it to work and snuck upstairs, trying not to be noticed so I wouldn't have to explain my erratic lateness. I went on, just as normal, trying desperately hard not to think of the dream, the mirror. How long ago had it been? A few weeks? Days? Last night? If anything, I was just fatigued. Simple as that.

I only managed to hear bits and pieces from news clips, reports on investigations... The Madison Police Department accruing more evidence or narrowing down details about this "alleged" serial killer business. Something like that, like I really cared. I had other, more important matters in my life to attend to. Like me.

My job was asking so much work of me, I had meetings to go to right and left, people were calling to set up times to go and "party"--even my mother (I love the bitch, I really do) was trying to set me up with Mr. I-Need-To-Blow-My-Load-In-Some-Pussy-Pretty-Soon...the week went on rather smoothly, or so I thought.

Susan didn't seem to particularly enjoy talking to me anymore, which was fine. I didn't even like the fake ass bitch to begin with. Part of me wanted to shove her head through my computer screen, watching the glass shards rip her flesh off, then take paper clips and ram them repeatedly into her eyeballs, popping them, watching the dark jelly ooze out slowly. I then wanted to shove post-it notes into her mouth, making her eat as many as possible; filling her up with all the fluorescent nonsense she seemed to fill everyone else up with.

But, I didn't. I was just normal enough. Okay, so I forgot to turn in a few case files here and there. I was about two hours late to the meeting, but hey, at least I showed up, the fuckers. Ungrateful little shits, seems to be a trend in the office--everyone's an ass-hole. Still, business wise, the office was running well. The only thing was the police were now interrogating everyone and anyone over who saw Lucy, or Laney, or what's-her-face last. People seemed scared, even Diane wouldn't go into the lady's room to take a shit by herself. Pathetic. Still, I carried on with my job like some determined work whore. Sure, I had been questioned a few times, but hey, those fucking pigs had nothing on me.

"Miss Ellis, did you know you're bleeding?"

"Huh?"

"You're uh...bleeding. On you hand."

"Oh! Oh yeah. I uh... cut myself. By accident, I uh, accidentally dropped my mirror."

"You look a bit pale. We can conduct this 'interview' later."

"I wasn't aware I was being interviewed, officer Garby."

"It's Gradly. And it's not an actual interview per se, it's, we just need to ask a few questions on the disappearance of Lisa Thatcher."

"Who?"

The officer in front of me, sitting rather casually on the plush, crushed red velvet guest chair I kept in my office-like cubicle, watched me silently. Did disbelief cross his intense features? My mother would call him, "a fine little looker, with a real big cooker". I however, didn't find his green eyes or black hair, or straight, masculine features attractive whatsoever. To be quite frank, he was wearing way too much cologne, and I was sure that he purchased his loafers from Payless or Target. Why couldn't I get a female cop?

I stopped my train of thought. Why would it matter if the damn pig was a girl or not? A small voice seemed to hiss in the back of my mind

(*dike*)

some slur that I couldn't quite make out because I was too busy staring at the officer's plaid tie. He was making me sick, if not violently ill. I blinked, realizing that I took way too long to redeem myself in any answer

now; I paused, but didn't freeze, not exactly.

"Miss Ellis, are you sure you're feeling
all right?"

"I think I might need that band-aide."

"Of course..." The officer leaned back, his
green eyes glued to me. I slid my hand over
my desk and fumbled with opening my drawer.
Once it was open, all that was inside were a
few pens and post-it notes. And apple cores.
Rotten, decayed, brown, gooey apple cores...
when? How did those get there? I stopped,
trying to remember, trying to think.

Someone was in my fucking desk! I thought
vehemently. *It's a MESS! An absolute mess!*

I glanced up, a small smile playing across
my pale lips. I had

(forgotten)

not put any lipstick on today. I searched
through the hoards of apple cores in my desk,
my fingers getting covered with brown oozing fruit pulp. At least my desk had a fresh
scent...sort of. I finally found a small package of band-aides that I kept there in case
of paper cuts, hang nails, etc. I don't to go
about leaking my blood on reports and files
and such--how unprofessional would that be? I
pulled one band-aide out and put it across my
palm. The sight of my own blood was making me

(horny)

unsure, and my hands were shaking. I felt
that damn cop's eyes on my every move. Finally, I finished the ordeal, feeling like it
had lasted for over an hour. I glanced to the
clock--oh good, it only lasted for about seven
minutes.

"All better?" The police officer asked. He

popped a mint into his mouth.

"Could you please swallow that? Or spit it out?"

"Hm?"

"The mint. I can't be inside closed spaces with mints--it bothers my sinuses."

The officer chuckled. Did that fucking, cock sucking bastard think I was kidding? My face was set perfectly straight, watching him rather intensely now. His chuckling died out almost instantly, and like a good dog, he swallowed.

"Okay, Miss Ellis, the intern that was hired about a month and half ago, Lisa Thatcher, she has been reported missing for nearly two weeks now. Have you seen or heard anything that might explain if she decided to leave? Or if you..."

"Nope."

"I'd like to finish my question."

"I thought you said this wasn't an interview."

"It's not."

"Fine. Continue." I was pressing on the cuticles of my nails, making sure they were shoved back as far as they could go so the whites at the bottoms of my nail bed could be seen clearly.

"Did she mention if she was leaving? Upset? Or going on vacation?"

"Not that I recall. We didn't know each other too well, officer Bartly."

"Gradly."

"Look, fine, okay. I'm just really busy now. You see, I practically own this company and when you have several different projects on your head at once everyone begging for your

artistic point of view, like you're some fucking God, it's hard to be up-to-date with every
little minuet thing. Can you possibly understand what I mean? Have you ever been demand-
ed from by multiple people all at once, all
expecting a phenomenal outcome by the time the
dead line is up? Have you?"

"Yes, Miss Ellis."

"Oh yeah? Explain."

"I'm working on this case."

"Oh." I looked down at my nails. They
looked ratty, uneven, slightly dirty. I didn't
know if the blood caked under the nail bed was
someone else's, or mine.

"Look, Miss Ellis, clearly right now is not
the best time to conduct a...*questioning*,"

I arched a dark brow.

"Right now." The officer went on, undis-
turbed by my obviously perturbed expression.
Fucker. "So, how about I leave you my card
and I'll simply reschedule a time to speak
with you, huh? And if you hear or see anything, feel free to call at any time."

"I disconnected my telephone."

The cop watched me. Was he *gauging* me? Was
he checking me out? The fucking nerve of this
pervert, Jesus Christ.

"Well, then you can use your office phone,
or something, Miss *Ell*is."

"Don't accentuate the "L's"; I hate it when
people do that."

"You seem to have a lot of dislikes."

"What's that supposed to mean?"

"Just an observation."

"Yeah? Well don't. I think you know how to
vacate from the premises now, Mr. Grady."

"Fair enough." He stood up, adjusting his

suit some. I couldn't help but once again send another scowl at his loafers and then I spun back to my desk once he was gone. I took out two moldy apple cores and meshed them together--I made something that either resembled the ancient Pyramids, or, oddly enough, Charlie Chaplin. I then set the rotted fruit cores on my desk, on top of a few papers. Paper weights.

Fear no art.

I had decided to show up to my local gym (I couldn't remember the last time I had gone, to be quite honest) and headed to my old locker. I had left a change of freshly cleaned gym clothes in there, and not caring if anyone was looking or not, I changed, stripping my work clothes off and slid into my gym clothes.

"Good God, Sam, what happened?"

"Huh?" The twitch in my eye would be a permanent--I'd never get used to people just freely using my name whenever they felt like it. The insignificant morons obviously had no idea just *who* I was, or how powerful I was. My name was not something to just throw out there and use like some condom. I did all the fucking work, I deserved a bit of respect, but since idiots happened to populate the world more than the intellectuals (why is it that horrendously stupid people seemed to multiply like rabbits and smart people were so scarce?) I guess I'd play the "game" and put up with my label. If society needed to feel a bit better about labeling *every* shithead thing, then so be it.

Still, I couldn't help the twitch of my eye.

"I said, you look cut up real bad. I think

you're bleeding. Are you okay?"

"Of course I'm okay, Janey."

"Janey?"

I glanced up. It was my work-out partner... what was her fucking name? She was the walking tooth-pick, mismatched eyes, God what was it?

"What happened?! Look at you. I'll grab some banda--"

"NO MORE BAND-AIDES!" I screamed out. "It's NATURAL and good to bleed sometimes. Besides, I heard that in India they purposely bleed to create body art. I'm an artist. I was trying a new form of..."Then the TV behind her caught my eye.

Janine turned her head to glance at the TV screen in the gym room. The music videos had been interrupted once again to show another news update.

"Detective Clairmont stated Wednesday that now he has a few leads. He was unable to comment on who and where these supposed leads may be located. However, Detective Gradly had this to say..."

The TV then switched scenes from the horse-faced news anchor woman (people as ugly as her ought to simply be dragged out to a field and shot. Put out of their misery) and showed the *exact* same fucking cop that had been to my office earlier today to interrogate me.

"We feel that we're getting closer to our suspect. This city will begin to feel safe once again as soon as Detective Clairmont and myself catch that one miniscule mistake."

"How are you so sure of the serial killer making a mistake, Detective Gradly?" came a question from some reporter at the press conference.

"Because their greatest fault is the fact that they're insane."

"That's what I've always said." I whispered to myself.

I glanced away from the TV, catching Janice, Jamie--whatever, looking at me rather apprehensively.

"Are you really okay?" She asked me again. I had my shirt on, I started to pull on my shorts.

"I SAID yes, or are you fucking deaf as well? Open your Goddamn ears, okay? I don't exactly have time to sit here and discuss life stories. You must understand I'm a woman who's in *very* high demand. Can you comprehend that, or would you like me to go slower? Perhaps place it in laymen's terms...in other words, fuck off and shut the fuck up, you're lucky just to be in my presence."

I don't think I'd ever found out if her contact in her left eye was simply dry, therefore making her eyes water--or if I had made the stupid bitch cry, which, in her case would be a fashion no-no. Her makeup would smear down her gaunt, bony little cheeks (Christ, the woman needed some meat on her…) and pool about the rims of her eyes. She'd look like the biggest crack-whore to hit the streets, or, Tammy Faye Baker, --who probably was the biggest crack-whore to hit the streets.

Still the woman with the "J" name walked off in a huff, not bothering to apologize to me for wasting my time with her insubordinate thinking. I headed over to my excercise machine and stepped on, setting up my standard run for 3.8 miles. The music videos on MTV were brought back on again and I looked away, wanting to keep my own superior brain cells, rather than burning them out on some fucking musician's sex video. They disgusted me.

There was that whole argument that went on between parents and their kids, and society. Does TV and music make children violent? Desensitize them? Well, how does one determine violence, huh? Here we had people who are so gung-ho about war, capital punishment, guns, and yet, we blamed the kids because it was what they are watching on TV?

NEWS FLASH!

Where the fuck were the parents, huh? If those shit heads were actually doing their jobs, rather than going out bar hopping, raping kids, having affairs and getting hopped up on drugs and alcohol, maybe little Johnny or Suzie would show a bit more respect.

Then again, my mother was always there for me. Always. Did she abuse drugs? Go and fuck every man from here to Timbuktu? Was I raised on the cheesy gore/horror flicks of the '70s? No. None of those things applied to me. I would love to give an episiotomy to the thin flesh right above the asshole of whatever scientist came up with these absurd studies and insane data about why people commit murders or partake in taboo behavior. THEY DID NOT PORTRAY TRUTH!

Besides, I had never watched a music video in my life.

I casually glanced around, not taking note of anyone else in the gym… I was actually looking for…

STOP! My heart rate quickened. I hadn't seen that decayed girl, the voice, since the

night of the dream.   I thought maybe she had
gotten the point to leave me the fuck alone-
-good for her.   The voice was actually kind
of smart, she listened when she was told to.
And she brought up some interesting, artistic
points.

STOP IT!!!

She was gone, the voice was gone, like I
wanted.   I smiled broadly, and for once I was
actually listened to, for a split second as it
was taking time to collect my thoughts, the
lyric of some weird song came to me ironi-
cally enough.   Go figure music would now play
some sort of factor in my thoughts... "All the
lonely people, where do they all come from?"

Under my breath I muttered as a sweat broke
out on my forehead, "We come from the truth."

18

7:19PM

I was taking a small walk outside of my apartment complex. Things in the office now were all quieted down. I hadn't been to my gym in weeks since that "J" named bitch and I had some "falling out." Basically it resulted in me threatening to cut her green eye ball out and feed it to her, then piss down her throat and suffocate her with my cunt. Yeah, like I said, I hadn't been to my gym in weeks.

The trash burning system was still down at my apartment, and I think I remembered reading a notice that it was going to be abolished due to all the pollution. Who were all these ass-holes who cared about the fucking environment? That was an inconvenience to me as a citizen, and it shouldn't be. Let someone else's kids deal with a dirty earth. It was not my fault that the earth was polluted to the point where it would only be able to sustain life for a couple of trillion years, rather than a few quadrillion. Boo-mother fucking-hoo.

My apartment was thrashed and trashed. Clothes were everywhere. I smeared the rest of that girl with the "L" name's intestines all about the carpet. I sawed off part of her skull and covered it in glass enamel--leaving half of her brain beneath the coating of glass, and turned it into a cereal bowl, to join the two others that I had like that.

I used the large femur bones in the legs to create a magazine wrack, but the wrack was too big, so it became my shoe wrack. I ripped out as many salvageable teeth I could and glued them together--making them a door stopper. The rest of her mutilated, decayed, rotting body I just drug all about my apartment like some puppy with its brand new toy.

Blood and entrails oozed on my carpet, over my couches, on my walls. Things were stained, and blood never comes out, not completely anyway. I cut off the girl's hair completely and washed it. I then fixed it permanently to a hair-tie, making a homemade hair piece. I did rather well, actually. I'd have given it to that fake bitch at my work…the "S" girl, if she weren't such a bitch.

Though my walk was short, it helped to clear my mind. Time and people were so shifty lately. The night I had unplugged my phone, I had never plugged it back in again. I lived by my cell phone, and even then I was not answering any of my calls.

I headed out of the small courtyard from my complex, a light rain drying up. The rain fall was so slight, if anything it just felt good on this cool night. For whatever reason, I had been awfully hot, and nights like these, I simply loved. I walked down the sidewalk, my eyes glancing up towards the sky plunging sky scrapers. The city seemed so ominous to me, each and every building holding a room, and each and every room holding a secret.

Some lights flickered on and off, other lights stayed on, and others were off, and this made for twinkling buildings. The scents of pollution and people were in the air, as well as rain, yet no one was outside. At least, it didn't seem like it. It was funny, y'know? A city filled with so many people, and yet they all went out of their way to be alone. I guess, if I wanted to lower myself to their level by trying to understand why they chose to avoid other men and women, I would say it was because everyone had their own little life. No one wanted to be involved in someone else's drama, pain, love, ideas--their *feelings*. They simply just didn't understand *feelings*, whereas I do. I made the choice to decide on which feelings to embrace and which ones to not.

"Excuse me! Excuse me, miss?" came a voice to my right. I was shaken from my reverie and glanced over my slender shoulder.

The woman before me caught my eye quite clearly once I saw her. She was cute, very cute. She had dirty blonde slightly flipped out hair and dark blue eyes. She was a bit thick about the hips and belly, but not bad. And her lips…good God, I could've sucked on them all day, they were so full and pouting. She was delicious. Luscious. I wanted her. That's the one, Mommy, the kitty cat in the window--I want *that* one!

"Yes?" I asked with a broad grin, pulling on the ol' slick as a mother fucker, routine. My eyes grazed over hers and down over her full bust, to her little belly and then down her legs. I leaned on my hip some, my stance laid back, casual--what people would call, "inviting".

"Can I get you to sign something for me?" She asked, and if she noticed my hungry eyes, she chose not to do or say anything about it.

"Depends on what I'm signin', darlin'. What is it?" I tucked a lock of black hair behind my ear, my grey eyes narrowed some at her typical city "college kid" style--slightly grunge, slightly gothic. She wore a chain belt, with metal bracelets and a ball-bearing necklace. I couldn't tell what brand of clothing she wore--could have been from the GoodWill, for all I knew. It was black, and on her curvy form, it was hot. She handed me a pamphlet. "Here's a pamphlet on my topic of protestation. I'm pro-choice and I'm trying to find other women who feel like they have the right to their own body--don't wanna' be owned by the government and all, you know."

"Ohhh, pro-choice." I then murmured. The whole abortion thing, that's right. "Well, I'd have to say I see nothing wrong with the execution of some little child that has no real memory of its life in its mother's womb. I mean, I can barely remember back to last Wednesday."

The blonde laughed gently and then shifted in her boots. "Yeah, though I wouldn't even call abortion an "execution." I mean, you're simply taking out the egg of what *might* be. An egg isn't human."

"True," I said pointedly. "But, they're made by humans so does that mean we ought to "abort" art? Technology? Books? All of those things are made by humans as well. In a sense, they're all "conceived", right?"

Clearly not offended, she seemed to be enjoying the intellectual conversion I was allowing her to have with me. Such a good little girl. "Well, yes they are but, art, technology, books, they don't spurn the power to go out and behave like an insane criminal in society. They may influence that kind of behavior, but they're not *living* entities, they are simply entertainment, kinda to, you know, pass the time by."

"Pass the time by?"

"Yeah."

"How do you mean?"

"Until we die."

"Well…heh, that's morbid."

"Yeah, but true," she smiled broadly. "Besides, I've gotta have an appreciation for "death" in life, especially if I'm out here, handing out abortion packets and collecting signatures."

"You've got a point," I said, nodding my head. I thumbed through the pamphlet, pretending to skim it. Honestly, I couldn't read a damn thing, all the letters looked like they were floating up and off the page.

The words then hovered up, rearranging themselves, right in front of my fucking eyes. I stared in disbelief, unable to look away, and watched as the words then spelled out:

S.O.S.

I'm sure that blonde didn't see this. Most people had a tendency to suddenly become blind when they were asked for help. I blinked, hearing her ask, "So, will you? Sign, I mean. Not to be offensive, but you strike me as someone who seems to have an idea about what's going on."

"Yes, I do. More than most," I had to agree with her. The girl didn't move her eyes from mine. I had her in the bag. I always landed whatever girl I sought out, it was like a gift from God or something. My gift to me. "But as far as signing, I don't know if I'm convinced enough. Are you aware how incredibly cliché it is for an artist to get political?"

"You're an artist?"

"Yes. An interior designer."

"Wait a second…" The college girl said, looking me at me very closely now. "You're that Ellis girl, right? The one who re-vamped the club over on Broadway? Harmonium?"

"Yeah. But don't do that."

"Do what?"

"Accentuate the "L's" in my last name. I hate it when people do that."

"Oh, sure. But wow, I read about that in the paper. You did a great job."

"I know, that's why I work where I do." I shot her a quick grin. This was getting to be a bit annoying now. I knew I was fucking good, talented--a fucking genius. I didn't need some low level thing like *her* telling me this.

"Okay, I get the whole "artist" comment then. But still, Ms. Ellis..."

My eye twitched.

"Would you like to sign? It's not like I'm gonna' exploit your signature, or anything."

"Right."

She held out the clipboard loaded with the signatures of other women on there. I paused… should I? Would I even dare to affiliate my-self? I glanced up, my eyes resting on the girl's predominant cleavage.

Whatever.

I took the pen from her and signed it. After all, I have no problem supporting the killing of unborn children. They'll only grow up to fuck up this world more so than it already is. Might as well spare them the agony now. Besides, they're incapable of thought, why would they even care if they lived or died at that age, regardless?

"Thank you so much Miss Ellis."

"Uh, call me…" I paused, call me what? WHAT? What could she call me that wouldn't annoy me, make me angry, enraged… what indeed. Get over it, dike it out, butch it up--just tell her your name. "Call me Sam."

"Okay, Sam." Her small smile told me that she was either: A) Grossed out for she is a girl being hit on by another girl. Or, B) Turned on so much that her nipples became so hard they could fucking cut right through glass.

Ding, ding, ding--answer B is the right answer in this case.

"Or," I started out, keeping complete eye contact with her. "You can just call me."

"Really?"

"Better believe it, darlin'." I was feeling giddy again suddenly. I was feeling…rejuvenated. FINALLY! I was starting to revert back to my old self. The ol' girl could feel again. "How much longer you working this gig tonight, anyway?"

"'Bout for another two to three hours."

"That long?"

"It's for a good cause."

"Yeah, the promotion of child murder."

She smirked and shook her head.

"Well c'mon, I mean, it's not like the world is suffering from under-population, anyway."

"You're bad."

I then leaned forward, feeling hungry like the wolf now. "And you like it," I flashed her a devious grin and she smiled back, blushing. "C'mon, if you left your post for like an hour, no one would know."

"But then I couldn't get my petition signed," the blonde countered, a few locks of her blonde hair sliding into her eyes. Christ, I wanted her!

"For only an hour. I'm sure people will be able to get on with their lives if a pro-choice supporter suddenly went "missing" while working."

She laughed then glanced over my shoulder. I reluctantly followed her gaze, simply spotting the backed up traffic on the streets, a cop car stopped at the red light.

"C'mon…" I prodded. She glanced around, as if she was getting ready to commit some terrible crime. "I live just right there." I pointed towards my apartment complex and she followed my direction. "We can get drinks, huh? Nothing more. That's all, and you'll be back in a jiffy."

"Well…"

"Come on, it'll be worth it."

She watched me for a long moment and instantly I pulled a large ridiculous grin on my face, making her laugh.

"Fine," she *finally* said. "But just for drinks and that's it. I really need to get back here."

"No problem," I said, my mind ticking like a

watch with a battery that had been soaked in a vat of liquid cocaine for a week. "I'll have your back in no time."

"Huh?"

"You'll be back in no time." Heh, right, "no time" at all. I wasn't lying, was I? We left her little protest post and headed back to my place. She made it up to the door and as the door opened, the scent of decayed bodies, fecal matter, bile, urine, mildew, mold, trash--everything, all hit her at once, I grabbed her like a mouse simply ready for the snake's taking.

She didn't even have time to scream as I slammed the side of her head against the wall and pulled her inside.

19

8:03 PM

When she came to, she was tightly tied up in the guest room's closet, bound and gagged. I heard her muffled cries as I was busy filling up an eye dropper with nail polish remover and caught the sight of that little blond suddenly before me. Granted, she was hot, granted, I would love to fuck her cunt raw and bloody… but, I wanted even more to watch the acid burn off her clit. I then wanted to sew her hole up with a needle and thread and shove my flexible shower head's tube up her ass, fill her up like some water balloon. Until she popped.

I finished filling the dropper and knelt down beside her, ignoring her muffled sounds then I spread her legs wide open (of course, I had stripped her of all clothing by now) and trailed the eye dropper down between her breasts. She squirmed beneath me, a wriggling little worm. Further down I trailed until I reached her small mound, she was a baldy down there, and this pissed me off profusely.

Not like I was in support of the Goddamn rainforest growing between your thighs, but I mean, fuck, a little shrub was nice to have. I smeared some and then, without parting her lips, I forced my hand inside. I violently shoved three fingers deep into her cunt, the eye dropper pushing up within her. I then squeezed, releasing the acidic chemical of acetone within. She was trying with all her might to scream, but the gag prevented her from making much noise at all. In fact, with a sickening "pop" sound I heard her dislocate the hinge of her jaw through clenching her teeth so hard on the gag.

The scent of chemically burned flesh was present, blood began to flow out as her skin started to deteriorate, eaten away, leaving small pink and red strings of fat. Tissues of the inner wall to her cunt began to chunk off and I finally pulled my hand back out. I tilted over and leaned against the guest bed. I had taken out my small box of "tools". From within, I extracted my eyelash curler (you know, it's that metal thing that looks like scissors that you saw your mother put up to her eye once her mascara was applied then crimped down on the lashes, making them seem longer? Fuller? Yeah, that thing...) and fixed the "scissor-like" end about the pearl of her eroded cunt.

I squeezed on that piece of ultra sensitive skin, clipping it off, making more blood ooze down. I watched her shudder and pulse beneath me, moving like how an animal moves just before it knows it is to die. My expression was just as silvery as that eyelash curler, both of us rather steely, cold. It was then that I decided to cut off both of her ears and use them to create a homemade phone. I intended to use her spine as the base of the phone. I would merely decorate my old phone, switch the wires out of it and place them all into my bio-phone.

I moved the eye curler up to her ear and began to clip at it slowly, not even thinking twice about the falling tears or moans of pain. The girl had tried to scream herself hoarse, and look where it got her?

CLIP!

Earless.

I tossed the bloody ear aside, more red, warm fluid now gushing down the side of that blonde's head. I moved back towards my box of "tools" and removed a sharpened razor. I carved on the cavity hole her "missing" ear had left. She convulsed. I moved like some automated robot. It was then I decided to scalp her as well. I could use her hair and scalp as part of my bathroom rug. I placed the razor against her forehead and pressed down, feeling the blade push through the first layer of flesh.

Her tears fell against the gag about her mouth and dripped onto the knees of my jeans as I knelt before her. I began to cut, blood pooling up and spilling down as I sliced her flesh open about her scalp, following the line as best I could. How the fuck did the Indians (and FUCK being politically correct, damnit! There are blacks, whites, Mexicans, Chinese, Japanese, and Indians! None of this "Native American" or "African American" etc. bull shit) make scalping look so DAMN easy? I began to rip her scalp up from her muscle layer, parts of her scalp tearing like paper, other parts seemed to be stuck to some spider web of a muscle. Finally I got half of her scalp off when I began to lose my focus on that.

I was everywhere at once. My thoughts popping about my brain like twinkling ornaments on the Christmas tree. Where the FUCK are my presents, huh? Don't tell me I was a "bad girl" this year--we liked to burn things with our coal you know.

Still, deep down…something, something, something… SOMETHING was lost. The game was lost. My pencil broke and I still needed to shade my sketch. After all, the eyes looked a little off…

I was in control, DAMNIT! I was doing things with order! I'd get back to her other ear to remove it…or… was that her finger? Whatever! I'd get to it, eventually. Didn't I mess with something else…? So much blood everywhere…

I dipped my finger into a pool of cooling blood and then lifted up my bloody first finger and wedged it up her nose. Her breathing rattled out feverishly, slowly suffocating by my penetration. I then ripped out with my finger shoved up as far as I could into her, at first hearing the skin tear, then the cartilage, then the muscle. Her nose not only broke, but with the force that I had yanked on it, it ripped right off. More blood, more spewing…and if anything, it was all one blur to me.

Ever hear the joke, "What's black, white, and red all over?" Want to know the punchline? "A penguin caught in a blender." I know, I never found it that comical either--I was just curious to know if the penguin was still alive when it was put into the blender.

I only feigned a smile when I saw the fear

and pain in her eyes. This was my fun. This was my art. My life. This was me, wasn't it? Wasn't it?

I wish I may, I wish I might, send me a true love. Now. Right now, mother fucker. Though if she could see this endless pleasure, this endless emotion and passion, and if I were to feel? Oh yes, but to feel again, to taste once more. Coming and going like a spring breeze, buying, destroying, loving and loathing, couldn't she see? Couldn't they all see? What was love, hate, fear, security? What was this…this disease, this gift of emotion? It all came from somewhere. And it must've gone to some place. Billowing out to somewhere.

Guess what, when I was inside out, upside down, or simply blue, that's when I found the secret to life. I was always and only okay when everything was not. Suck on that Einstein, Socrates, even my beloved Gwenyth Paltrow.

Suck it in you mother fucking cunt, and you breathe it out. You want this just as much as I do, huh? Huh? You want to be me? You want my pictures? My art? My say-so? I am GOD! I'm an artist. I create and I destroy--just like God. We're both artists, right? I KNOW GOOD AND BAD! I am not only just an artist--no. I am THE ARTIST! I give life! I make emotion! I am what you feel when you cry, sing, laugh, fear…this is me. And I'm you. You, you, you, and you. I'm you when you're screaming at the slow traffic in your car. I'm YOU when you fuck your wife. I'm you when you slap your husband for cheating. I'm even YOU when you stand up to your school bully for the first time. I am you when you sneak food into your bedroom after your parents said not to at two in the morning. I AM you. Don't you dare sell that short, don't you DARE tell me I am a liar…I simply act it out because I can, because I live the truth, because, you know it too. You feel it, you live it, you NEED it! YOU NEED IT! YOU NEED ME!

"YOU NEED ME!" At this point, I couldn't tell if I was thinking or screaming aloud. I just began hacking at her. Bits of flesh, fat, blood, muscle, all flew up and splattered all over me. I was crying as I hacked into her, losing everything all at once. I vomited on her as she lay beneath me, in the closet, twitching, taking her last few breaths. My bile seeped into her cuts, she could no longer writhe in agony, as I had assumed. She could only handle so much torture before she began to shut down permanently. I sobbed over her, not knowing why, not knowing WHY!

"WHY?!" I screamed at her, bile leaking down my chin, I could still taste my stomach in the back of my throat. Strangely it tasted of mucus and apples. "Y-you!" I stammered. "YOU KNOW WHY!!! TELL ME!"

Her silence met me, dealing me a deafening blow.

It was her eyes that did it.

I raised my hand to strike her over the face, to crack her skull into her brain, then I stopped. Through my teary gaze, I met her eyes. They were losing their life and I could see that…I could see the moment it was leaving her. Soon, she would be gone, and soon she'd be no different from every other corpse I've ever known. Soon, she would be gone. And soon, my life would have to continue to move on, with or without her.

I, Samantha Claire Ellis, was alone.

I was utterly alone.

"Can't you...?" I whispered, my voice shaky, watching her eyes slowly fade, her life slipping away right before me. "Can't you enjoy this too?" I leaned down, my lips brushing over hers. "Can't you stay a little while longer? I'm scared. I'm scared and I'm so fucking scared to be alone. Don't ever, ever leave me. I can't do this alone... not anymore. I'm so scared. I don't want to. Never leave me. Please? Please...?" I wrapped my arms around her. I held her close, rocking her against me with a fragile, compassionate touch. "Oh please, don't leave me, please talk to me. Tell me you love it as much as I do. Tell me you cannot live without this. The pain is so close to pleasure, tell me you need it like I do."

I guess I fit the stereotype of the artist, huh? I got into the whole "addiction" scene. And just what is addiction? According to American Heritage Dictionary, it reads as such:

ad•dict (∂-dîkt') *tr.v.* **-dict•ed, -dict•ing, -dicts**. To devote or give (oneself) habitually or compulsively: *addicted to alcohol.--n.* (âd'îkt). **1.** One who is addicted, esp. to narcotics. **2.** A devoted fan: *a soap opera addict.* [< Lat. *addictus,* bondsman, p.part of *addicere,* to sentence: *ad-,* to + *dicere,* to adjudge.]**--ad•dic'tion** *n.*--**ad•dic'tive** *adj.*

Except, I didn't do drugs and I rarely ever drank. Remember, I was a light weight--we established this at the beginning. I was addicted to my control. My art? Yes, in a sense. And the bad thing about addiction was that it was so damn lonely. I wanted to share it with others, but I couldn't. Why? Because it was MINE! Mine, damnit. Though I had always been into the arts, been into creating my own "universe", I guess I took it one step too far, huh? Like how addiction goes, it ends up becoming you. Then again, wasn't I always this way? Maybe I should cop-out and say the reason why I suffered from addiction was because I wanted to be unconditionally accepted for who I was. Bullshit. What I choose is my choice and the killer that was me had the propensity to exist in each and everyone one of you, if you let it. If you chose to embrace it like I did. I knew who I was.

I was alone.

I didn't even hear the break-in to my apartment, nor did I really feel the hands placed upon my shoulders. I was jerked up from the corpse I was cradling. Having that dead blonde all to myself, unable to stop crying and shaking. Then I was only vaguely aware of being lifted up.

Finally, those hands to grab me and offer me comfort had finally come, right? No, it was the police, storming in and invading my oh-so-humble abode. Invading my moment of privacy, my moment of complete solitude. One of the officers had started vomiting like mad. He was the one who had the daughter with the puppy dog. He was worthy of my smile.

The bastard didn't return it.

He just continued to lose his lunch all over my carpet. The smell was rather rank, which I didn't appreciate, along with the way I was handled roughly by two police yanking me out

of her arms and rudely out of my guest bedroom. They were shouting at me, shaking me
from this surreal stupor, yet I couldn't understand a word they were screaming.

I lost count of how many officers were now
pouring into my home, scowling at my works
of art, how dare they. I was so tired, but
I strived to look for her, the voice, in the
mirror. Was she coming too? Did they get
her? The voice had stopped coming around ever
since that night I had so long ago. I hadn't
seen her since. But I needed her now. I
needed the voice now! I was…hey, I was feeling something! I was feeling...scared and she
was the only one who would understand me. Who
could explain. She was the only one who had
ever been there for me. Where was she now?
Where did the voice go?! Was she rotting in
someone else's mirror? Computer screen? Reflection? I needed her. I didn't want to do
this alone.

I was taken outside, the night sky greeted me with its dark, velvet wrap. The city
seemed to twinkle obnoxiously at me. Like
it was winking because it knew some secret I
had failed to see through my time of artistic need. I looked away, suddenly, something
surged through me. I felt like I needed to
shout, scream, laugh, or cry, perhaps do all
at once, but I couldn't decide.

Then I saw her.

As I was being taken to the squad cars that
were lined up about my apartment complex, I
saw her walking. She was definitely not my
type, first off. Too thin, long black hair,
and very, very tan. However, she was holding
a black back pack with big, bold, white writ-

ing on it. She stopped to look at me, seeing the scene that was unfolding before her.

Apparently, all of my neighbors, including that older than dirt man with his stupid yapping dog, decided to come outside and watch me as though I was some ring-side spectacle. All of them whispering, "oo-ing and awing" over the ordeal. Some seemed utterly shocked, others looked scared. Some mad, some indifferent, some simply interested for the free entertainment. Look ma, I'm a star. I was a sight to see, especially being covered in vomit and blood (not my blood, mind you) and being escorted outside by about five cops.

Yet, out of all my apartment complex neighbors, the girl with the black back pack caught my attention. She stopped and as we looked at each other, I read that sign that stated so clearly on her bag:

FEAR NO ART

I smirked, that sudden upheaval of emotion flooding through me. I screamed out and somehow (I think I may have popped my shoulder out of place to get my hand free from its confinement) but I raised my hand up, mimicking the Hitler salute. The police were caught off guard for a split second as I made this bold move, saluting the girl. And what did I scream out?

"All hail modern art!"

I was then apprehended, rather forcefully and painfully and shoved into the back of a police car. I sat in the back seat, trying to remember the last time I was ever in the back seat of a car, if ever. I was always up front, and always, I was the driver.

If I could just say goodbye to the voice once more...

If I could just see that horrible car accident, somehow, I knew, that then everything would be alright.

"Miss Samantha Ellis, have you understood the rights that have been read to you?"

I looked blankly forward.

"Samantha Ellis!?"

"Don't do that," I barely murmured out. "Don't accentuate the "L's". I hate it when people do that."

20

In the Middle of the Morning, Afternoon, or Night, or Whatever

"So things look much better with her."

"Yeah?"

"She seems to enjoy our 'movie time' in the afternoons."

"*Seems* to enjoy? Of course she would, it's not like she has much opinion of anything else!"

"Now, there's no need to raise your voice…"

"I know, I know… It's just, Christ this is hard. Mind if I have a cigarette?"

"Smoking is not permitted within the facility."

"Shit."

"I won't keep you much longer. Basically I called you over here to tell you that Samantha--"

"She likes to be called, Sam."

"That *Sam* is doing just fine. After her procedure she has--"

"*Procedure*? For fuck's sake, call it what

it is! A fucking lobotomy."

"Mrs. Ellis, calm down."

"It's Ms. Ellis actually, my husband and I are… uh divorced."

"How about I just call you Trixie, okay? Formalities are a bit past us now. You can even refer to me as Henry, if you'd like."

"Yeah, okay, Henry."

"Regardless of Sam's lobotomy, we feel that she's making real progress from where she first initially started out. After all, it's rather difficult to classify the level of sociopath she is, not to mention her grandiose illusion complex intergraded with, well, what we've concluded as a severe psychosis of schizophrenia. However, since the latest treatment, she just didn't seem to be showing any improvement with any sort of psycho-therapy, medication, or hypnosis. Lobotomy was, at that stage, we felt to be the best solution. Since such a procedure she's been making some progress. Though complete rehabilitation is out of the question at this point; her nature of being was too far out of reach for our help when she arrived and still is too far out of reach now."

"I'll bet."

"Look Trixie, I know this is hard for you. You've lost a daughter, but she was *not* a well person. She murdered up to twenty-five women. I believe they may still be finding more bodies. Sam needed to be helped. She still needs to be helped."

"I know…"

"Trixie, here, would you like a tissue?"

"Do you have children, Henry?"

"I don't think that my answer is really relevant here."

"Just, please, answer me."

"No, I don't."

"Then call *me* crazy for loving her, okay? She's still my daughter, my flesh and blood. Every morning, for the past six months, I've had to wake up and come to some sick realization that my own baby girl is responsible for such… such satanic …"

"Here's a tissue. Look, I can see where you're coming from, and I assure you, with the way the court ruled, she is considered as criminally insane. We are treating as best the state will allow us."

"That girl out there, she is NOT my daughter."

"Did you ever really know your daughter?"

"How dare you? How dare you ask me such a wicked question? It's enough that I have to pay and profusely apologize, even move states to avoid the animosity I get for the terrible acts my Sam has committed, but to be questioned if I even knew her? Are you accusing me of being a bad parent? I've given her everything I could--Everything. A mother only wants to see the good; she only wants happiness for her child. When her child is a convicted serial killer? How do you think that makes me feel? I'll tell you. I feel as though I failed. Somewhere along the lines I really well... fucked up.

"Am I to blame? Maybe, after all I did give birth to her. But, I wanted her. I loved her. I still love her. She will always be my daughter and there's nothing I can do to change that, nothing. Sure, being a single mother I wasn't there for her as much as I'd

like to be. Maybe she was just lonely having to look after herself while I worked to
support us. Maybe she felt I didn't love her
enough. I could go through a million different maybes but that won't fix what's been done,
will it?"

"Trixie..."

"What you've got out there, in that psy-
chiatric ward, that mindless zombie, is not
the Sam I knew. Not the Sam anyone knew. When
she was young she was a good kid, a damn good
kid with a lot of talent and charisma to offer the world. She was... I dunno, perhaps a
little more efficient with certain things, but
I didn't think anything of it. I didn't know
to. A kid's going to be a kid, right? She was
perfect to me. I don't want to hear about her
"progression". Who are you kidding? We both
know there will be none. I think I'd like to
sign the papers."

"Trixie, I think perhaps there's another
alternative here. After all, your daughter is
in our legal care now."

"Correction, I brought these papers to prove
that I have her back in my custody. And because she is now legally mine as well as bio-
logically mine? This is my decision."

"Trixie, that solution is a rather permanent
one. Perhaps if we simply keep her here under
our care, then she will at least be around for
you to come and visit--"

"NO. How many lawyers and doctors do you
think I've already been through? She was an
apparent menace to society when she was "herself", and now? She's just like the living
dead. And, Dr. Winstein, I cannot bear to
think about that. Not when I know how cre-

ative, smart, and talented she was. Not when I know how opinionated, strong, and just held that certain sense of self confidence. She always was a leader. Always did her own thing and Christ, I was proud of my little girl for being that way. I admired her. That... that shell out there... she would rather die than live the way she is now. I know it and I know her. I want to sign the papers for her termination. Why else would I make a six hour flight out here? It wasn't just to see her sit on the couch, staring like some comatose victim at the TV screen. My Sammy was never a victim, doctor."

"Please Trixie, I implore you to just think it over. Maybe give it a few days?"

"Do not call me by my first name, doctor. At this moment, I'd like to keep this formal."

"Understood."

"I have done all the thinking I need to do, Dr. Winstein. Respect that. I want to sign them today and then donate her body to science. I'm not reconsidering."

"Are you sure?"

"If you ask me once more, I will get my lawyer over here to sue you for not complying with the legal guardian's wishes. If I know her at all, she would not want to live out the rest of her life like this."

"If that's what you wish Ms. Ellis, I'll grab them out from the file right here. But let me make this clear, once you've signed, it's permanent, no going back. Once your name is on that bottom line, Samantha Claire Ellis will be put to death by lethal injection in about three months from now. Are you aware of this?"

"Yes. And if you ever contact me again to prolong the due date or something, you WILL see me in court."

"I understand, Ms. Ellis. And now that you've signed, expect one more phone call the week before your daughter's execution."

"I will."

"Good bye, Ms. Ellis. Thank you for coming down here to see us, we still appreciate it."

21

Sometime During the Night, or Day, or Whatever

They said the movie today was a "good" one. They said I would like it. They said it had an actress in it by the name of Gwenyth Paltrow. They said I used to like her. They tell me I'm good at listening. Okay. I listen. They say a lot of things.

Sometimes I listen, sometimes I don't. They say I sit nice and quiet on the couch when the movies start. Okay. They said my mother was here to see me, and she was. She said she loved me. Okay. I just watched her. She said that I would always be her little girl. Okay. I didn't know I was little.

My mother also said that this would be her last good bye to me. Okay. She then started to cry. I just watched. They said my mother then had to leave. Okay. They said it was time for a movie. Okay.

I was led to the couch, they turned the TV on. I watched quietly, my eyes focused on the screen. I watched it for a long time, not really remembering anything of what I saw. Sometimes other people would laugh at scenes in the movie, sometimes they wouldn't. I was silent.

I do remember a scene where there was a blonde girl in the bath tub, smoking a cigarette and talking to her mother. They told me the name of the movie was, *The Royal Tenebaums*, and they said that Gwenyth Paltrow was the blonde girl in it. Okay. She was sitting in the bath tub, smoking a cigarette and talking to her mother. Oh yes. I said this. Right next to the bath tub was a small TV duct taped to the radiator, and still plugged into the wall so the blonde girl could watch her TV shows while she bathed. Okay.

The mother said to her daughter, "Well, I don't think it's very intelligent to keep an electrical gadget on the edge of the tub."

The daughter said back while still taking a bath in the tub, "I tied it to the radiator."

People laughed. Okay. I watched still quietly, not remembering much more except for one other scene. The same blonde girl, the daughter was talking to a small child about her missing finger. She had it apparently been cut off in a wood cutting accident. The child asked her why she had a finger missing on her hand, and she told him of the accident.

The child then said to the blonde girl about her finger, "Did you try to sew it back on?"

The daughter responded, "Wasn't worth it."

More people laughed. I watched. Okay. My days are easy. I wake up, and someone dresses me. I am then led down to the dining room where I have breakfast. I then am led outside to go on a walk. I then am led back inside and into the rec room to watch the others play cards. I then am led to the dining room for lunch. I then am led into the TV room to watch a movie. I then am led to the rec room again to watch the others play more cards. Then I am led back into the dining room for dinner and pills. I then am led into the bathroom and someone helps me shower. I then am led to my bed. Sometimes someone helps me use the bathroom. They say I don't know how to do it anymore. Okay.

Sometimes someone also has to wipe the drool from my lips because I don't know how to do it anymore. Okay. Someone has to help me brush my hair because they said I cannot do it anymore. Okay. All my days are like this. Okay.

Things are done for me because I don't know how to do them. I never really talk. I can't remember most of the films they let me watch in the TV room--only sometimes I do and sometimes I don't. I don't think I ever saw that woman come back who said she was my mother. Okay.

They say to me that I have one night left in my room before I am to be moved. Okay. No one else really speaks to me, but I can still hear them talk. And just before my medication is dropped into my Dixie cup, they say it is to make me go to sleep. Okay.

Quietly something…something quietly…

A thought they *hadn't* given me, hadn't told me about slipped inside. So quietly, so silently… somewhere I think I heard once, that the good die young. I am only twenty-nine.

About The Author

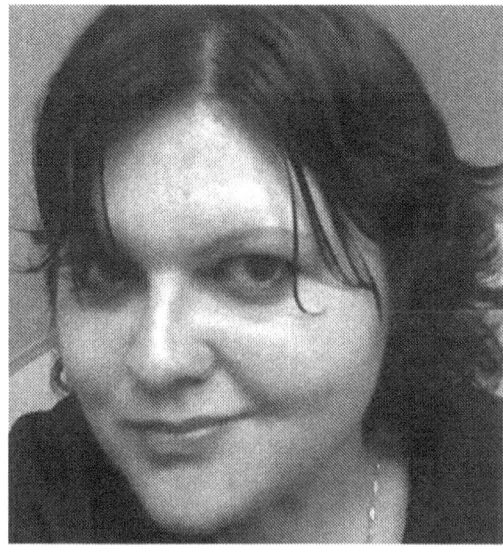

Heather Parsons is a twenty-one year old native of the boiling desert landscape that is known as Arizona. Upon graduating high school she is now attending community college part-time and works full-time. Obviously, she enjoys writing and upon putting out this first book she intends to do many others. Being able to create a world in which the reader can escape into and believe is her biggest passion. She writes anything from stories to darker areas of life, to award winning children's plays. After all, everyone has a story to tell, she enjoys telling them.

www.ingramcontent.com/pod-product-compliance
Lightning Source LLC
Chambersburg PA
CBHW032005170526
45157CB00002B/555